BUILDING BLOCKS OF ENGLISH

SENTENCES AND THEIR PARTS

Written by Jeff De La Rosa

Illustrated by Ruth Bennett

WORLD BOOK

a Scott Fetzer company
Chicago

T0407225

This edition is co-published by agreement between World Book, Inc. and Cherry Lake Publishing Group

World Book, Inc.
180 North LaSalle Street
Suite 900
Chicago, Illinois 60601
USA

Cherry Lake Publishing Group
2395 South Huron Parkway
Suite 200
Ann Arbor, MI 48104
USA

WORLD BOOK STAFF

Editorial

Vice President
Tom Evans

Senior Manager, New Content
Jeff De La Rosa

Curriculum Designer
Caroline Davidson

Proofreader
Nathalie Strassheim

Graphics and Design

Senior Visual Communications Designer
Melanie Bender

Library of Congress Control Number: 2024936274

Building Blocks of English
ISBN: 978-0-7166-5517-6 (set, hardcover)

Sentences and Their Parts
ISBN: 978-0-7166-5523-7 (hardcover)

Also available as:
ISBN:978-0-7166-5533-6 (e-book)

Cherry Lake ISBNs

Building Blocks of English
ISBN: 978-0-7166-8821-1 (set, softcover)

Sentences and Their Parts
ISBN: 978-0-7166-8795-5 (softcover)

Printed in the United States of America

Acknowledgments:
Writer: Jeff De La Rosa
Illustrator: Ruth Bennett/The Bright Agency
Series Advisor: Marjorie Frank

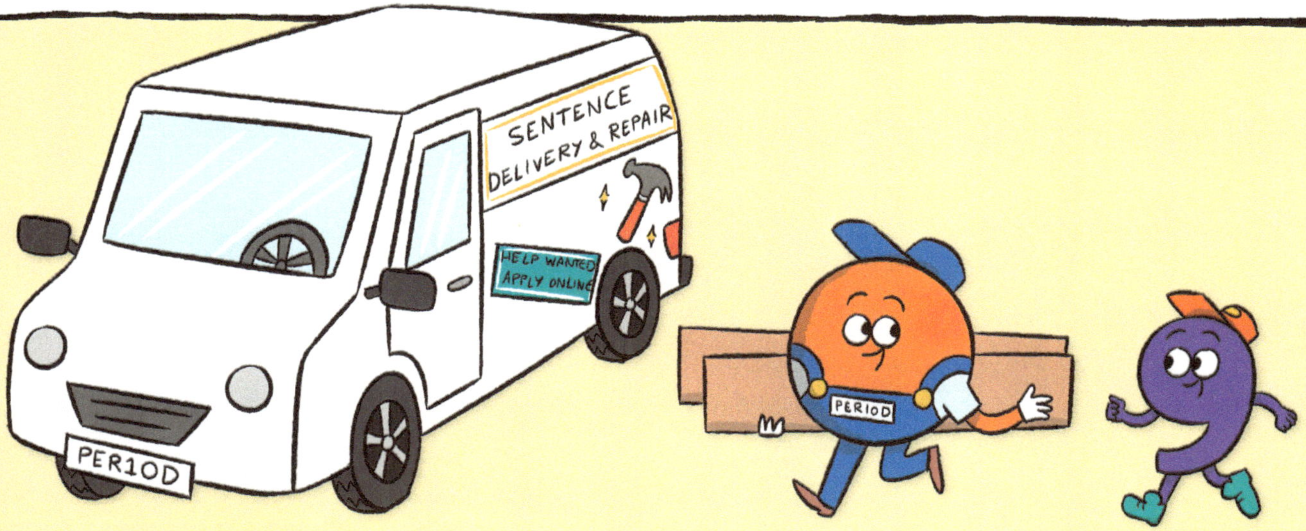
SENTENCE DELIVERY & REPAIR
HELP WANTED APPLY ONLINE
PER1OD
PERIOD

TABLE OF CONTENTS

There is a glossary on page 40. Terms defined in the glossary are in type **that looks like this** on their first appearance.

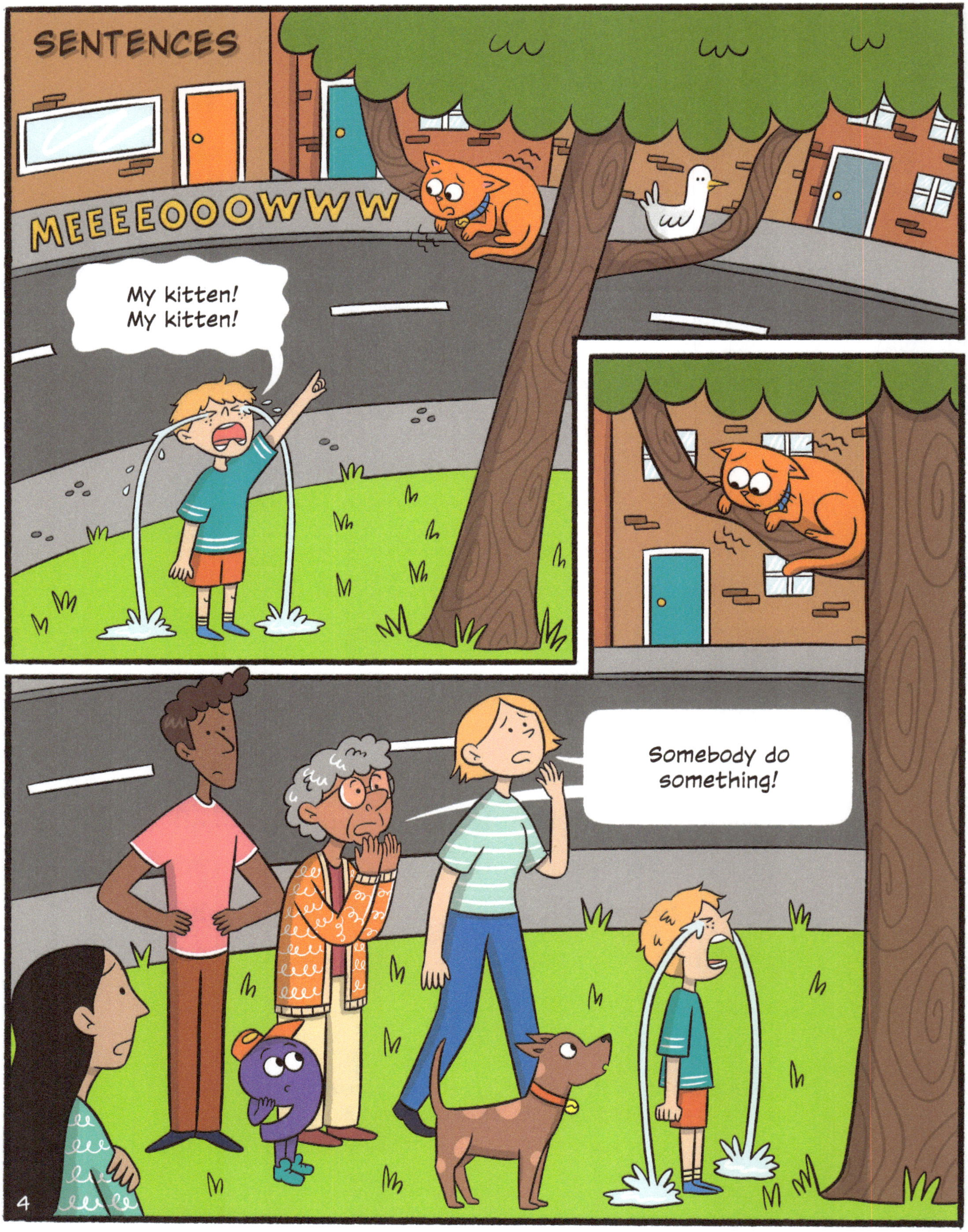
SENTENCES
MEEEEOOOWWW
My kitten! My kitten!
Somebody do something!

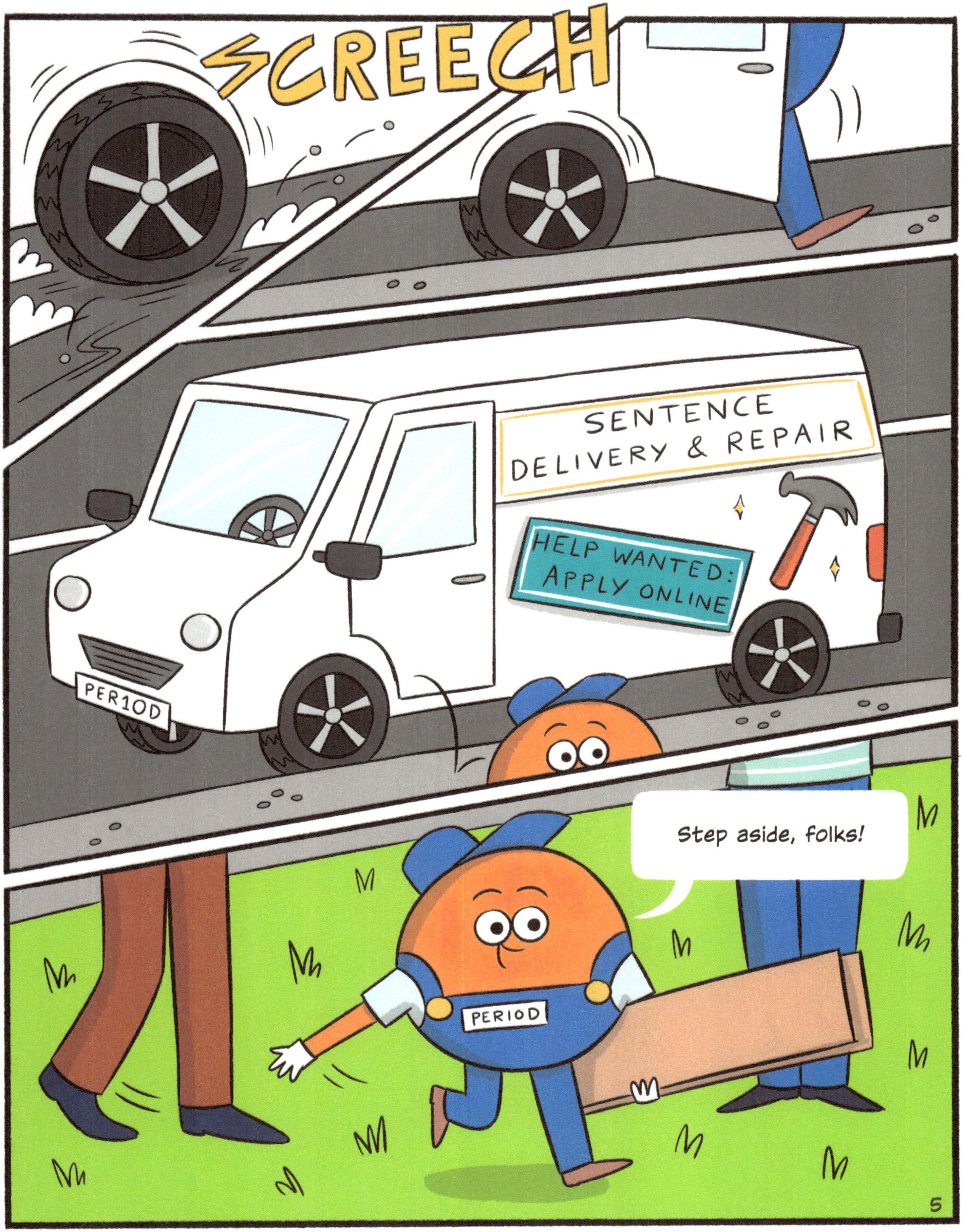
SCREECH
SENTENCE DELIVERY & REPAIR
HELP WANTED: APPLY ONLINE
PER1OD
Step aside, folks!
PERIOD

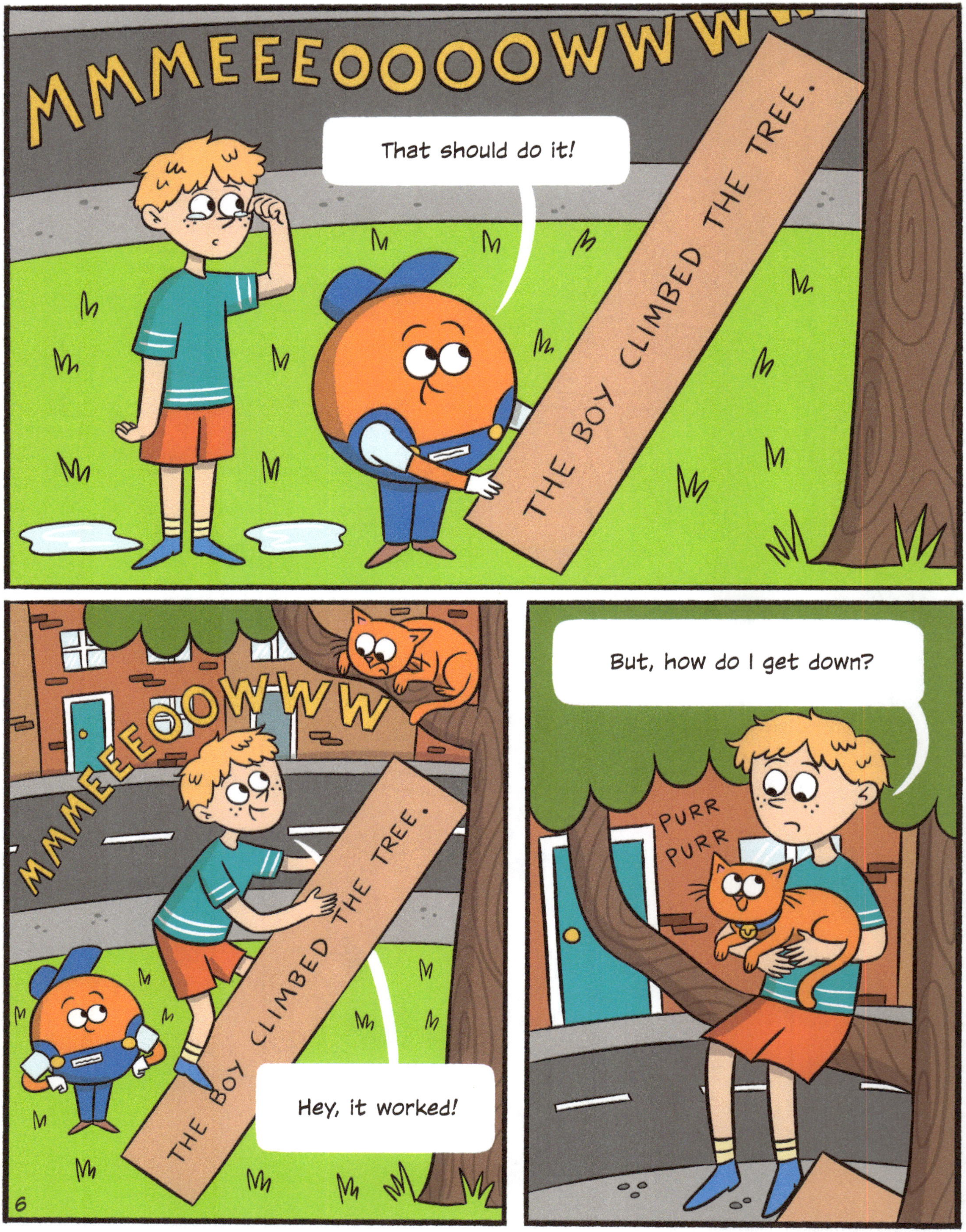
MMMEEEOOOOWWW
That should do it!
THE BOY CLIMBED THE TREE.
MMMEEEOOWWW
THE BOY CLIMBED THE TREE.
Hey, it worked!
But, how do I get down?
PURR
PURR

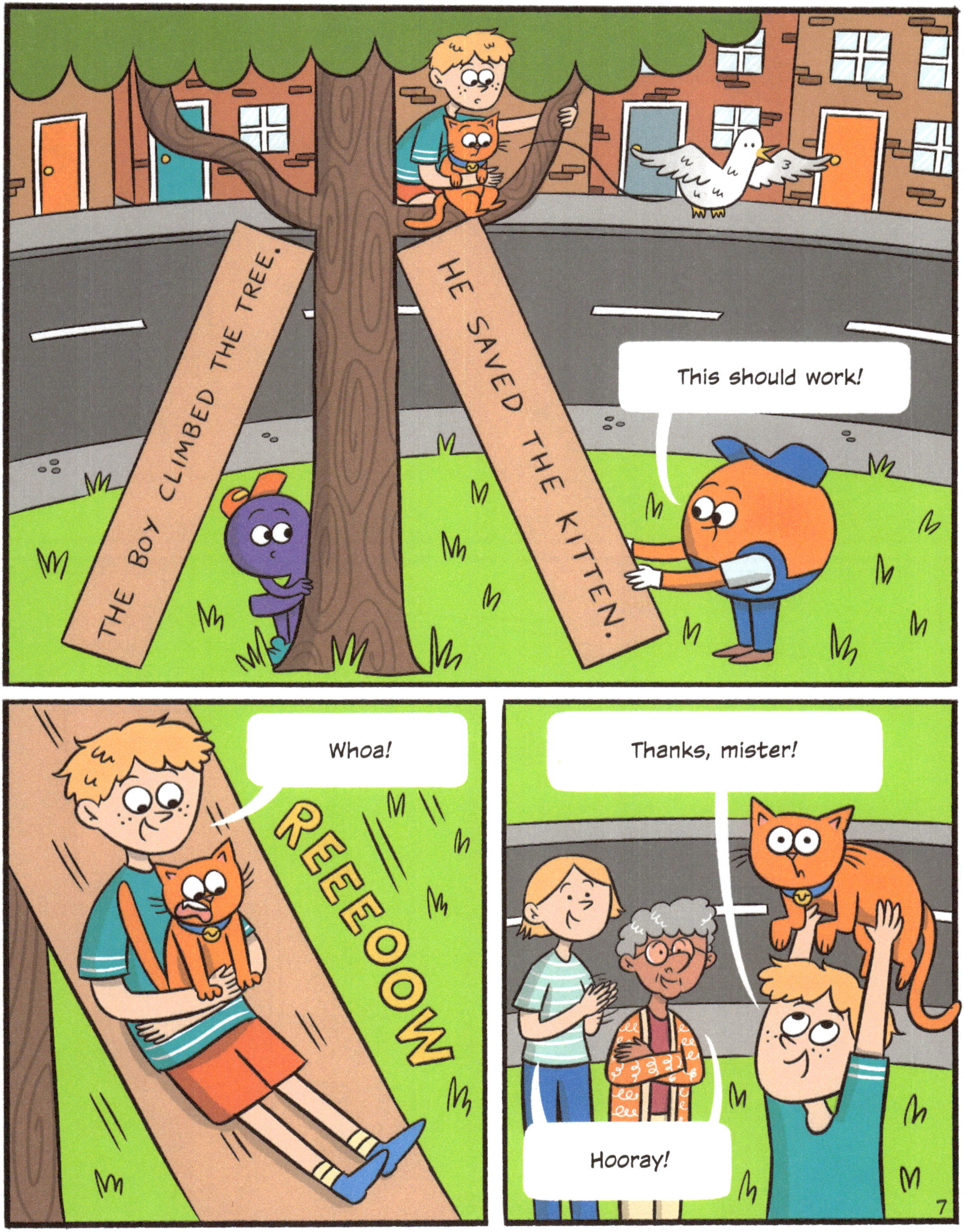
THE BOY CLIMBED THE TREE.
HE SAVED THE KITTEN.
This should work!
Whoa!
REEEOOOW
Thanks, mister!
Hooray!

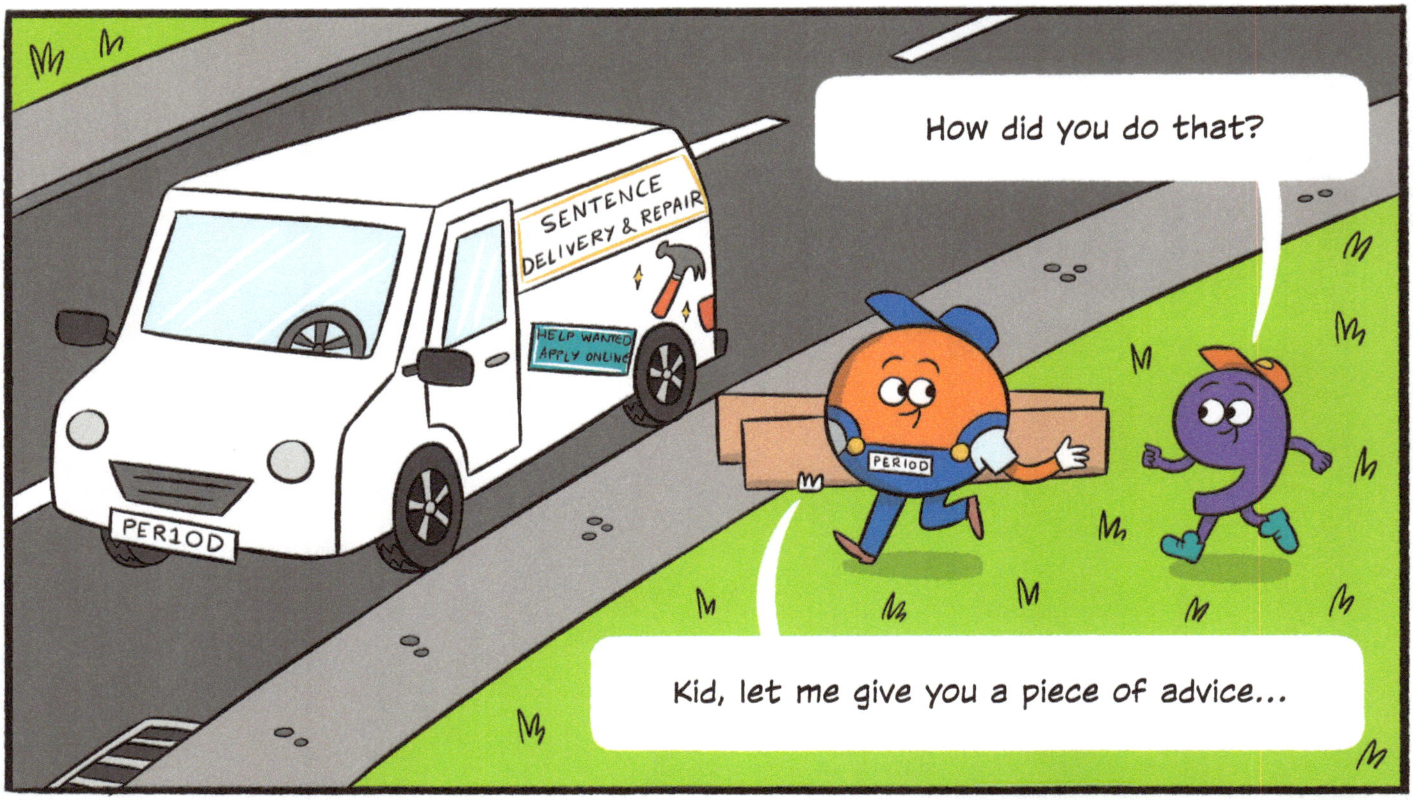
SENTENCE DELIVERY & REPAIR
HELP WANTED APPLY ONLINE
PER1OD
PERIOD
How did you do that?
Kid, let me give you a piece of advice...

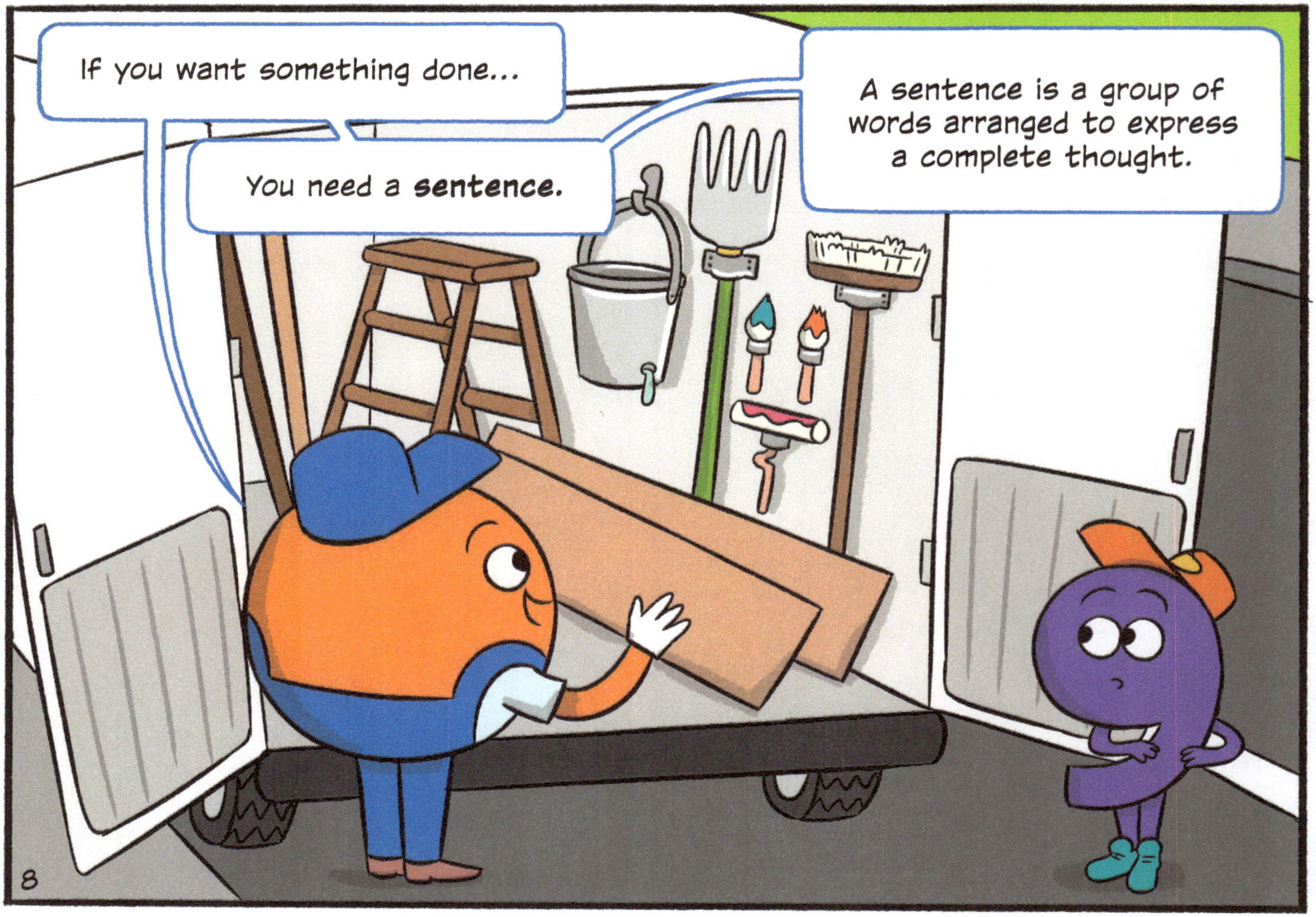
If you want something done...
You need a **sentence.**
A sentence is a group of words arranged to express a complete thought.

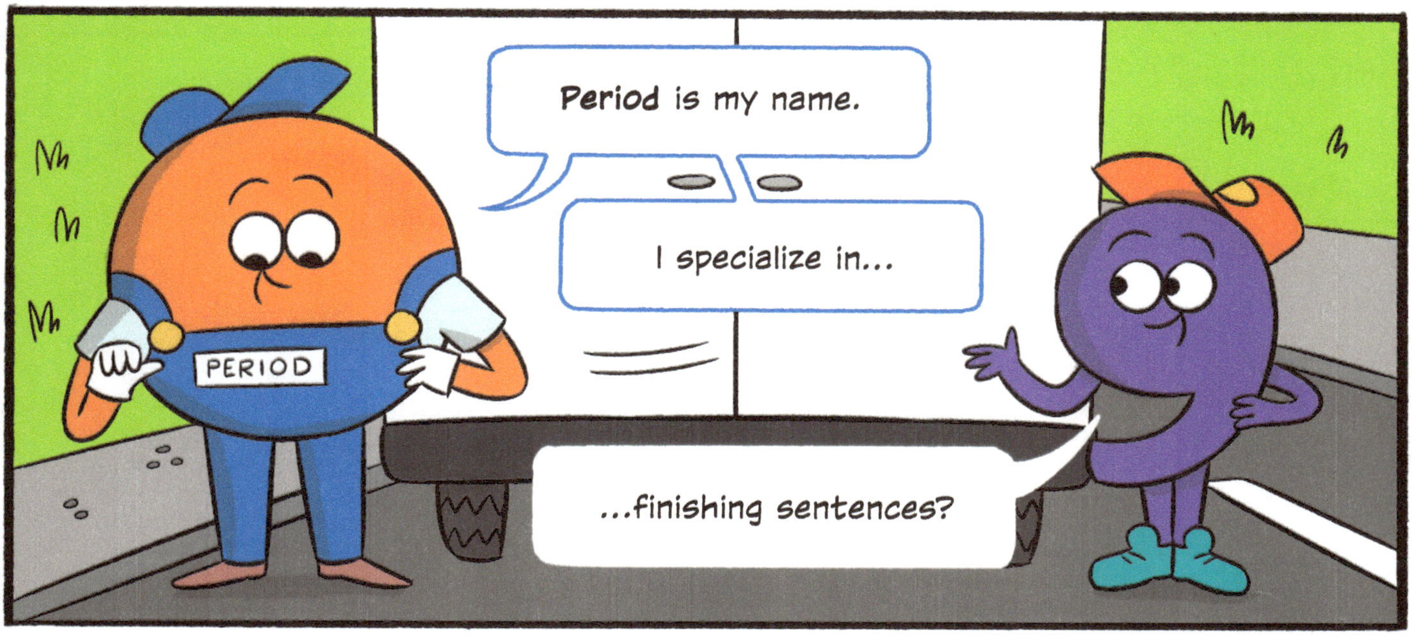
Period is my name.
I specialize in...
...finishing sentences?
PERIOD

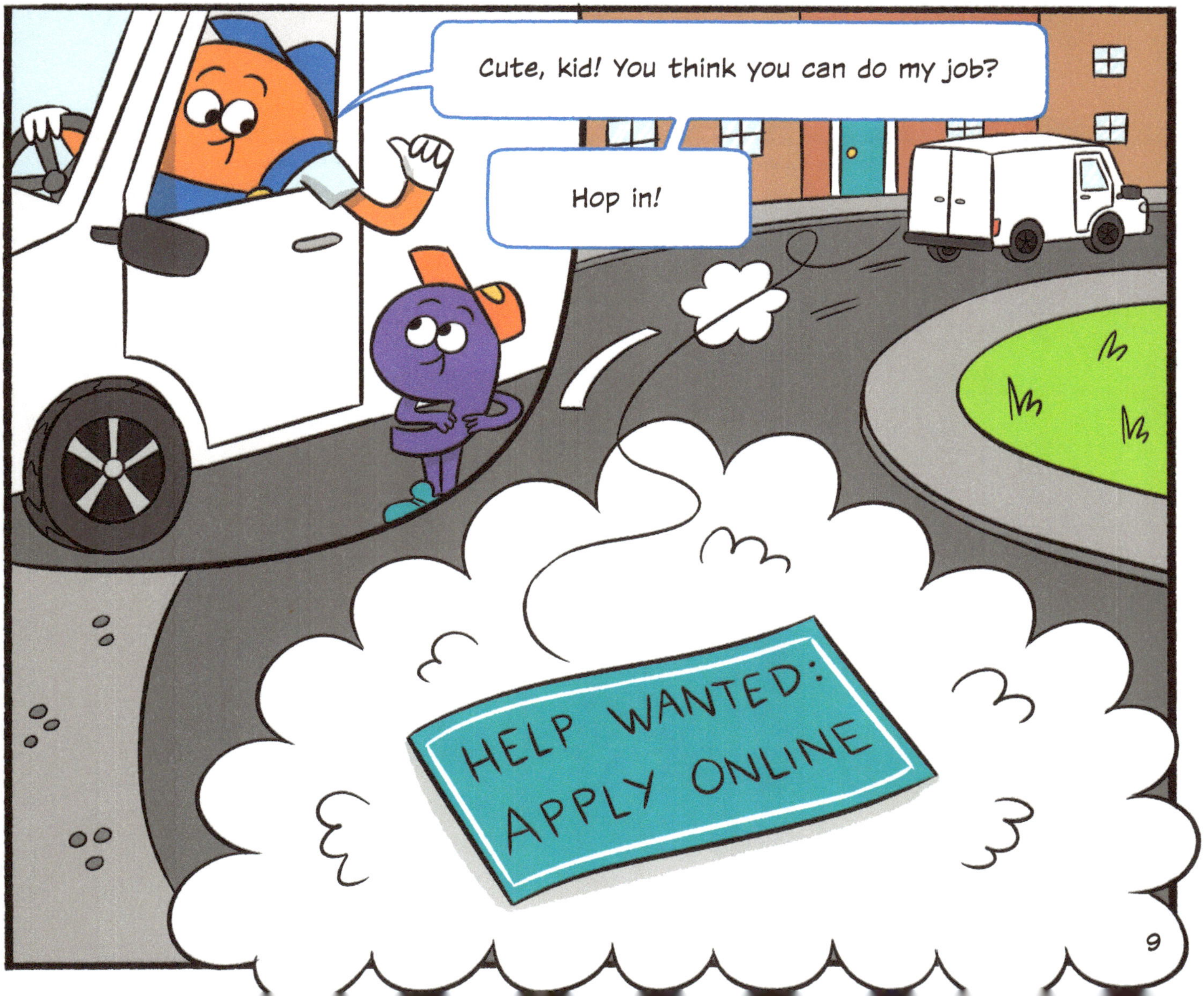
Cute, kid! You think you can do my job?
Hop in!
HELP WANTED:
APPLY ONLINE

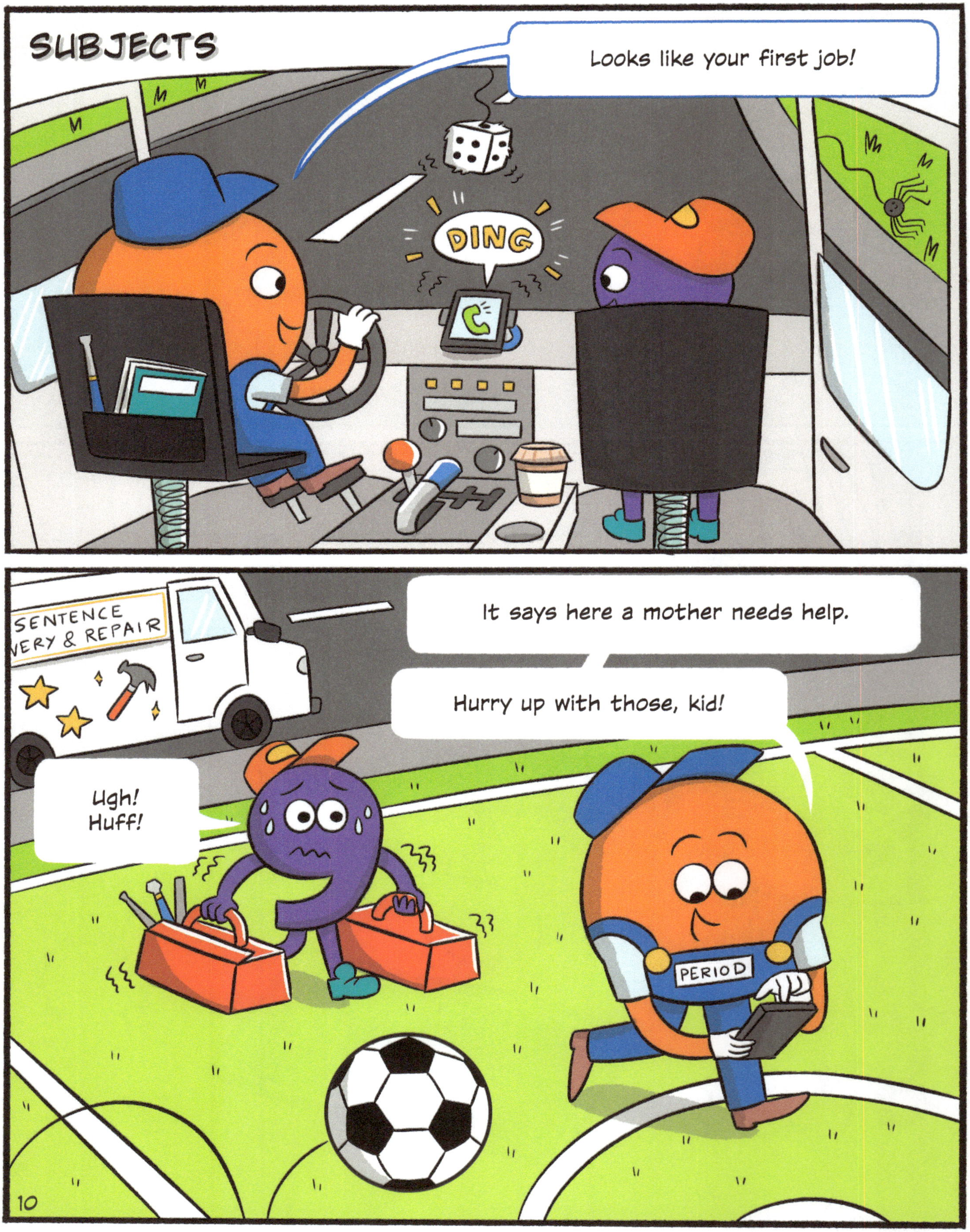
Looks like your first job!
DING
SENTENCE
VERY & REPAIR
It says here a mother needs help.
Hurry up with those, kid!
Ugh!
Huff!
PERIOD

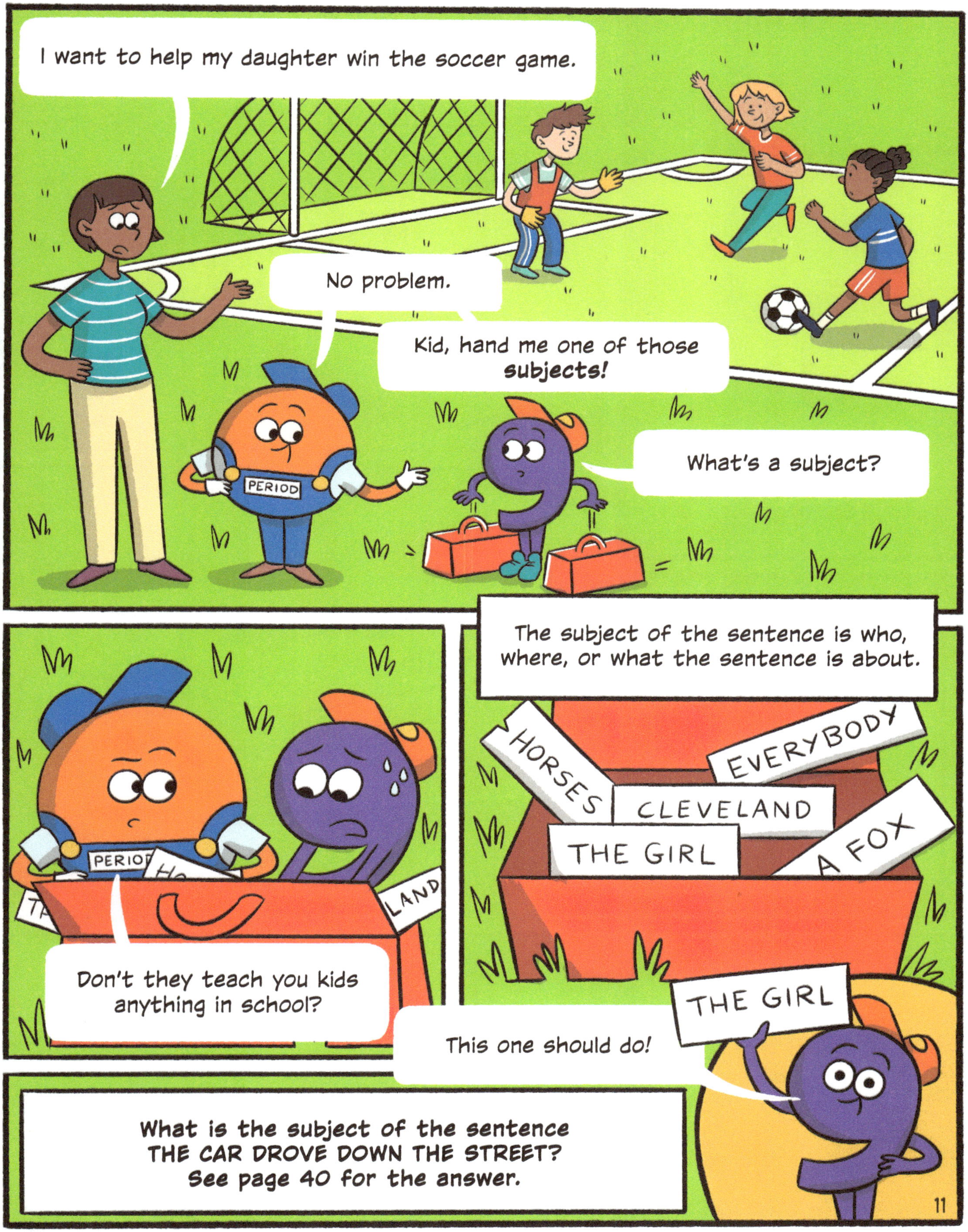
I want to help my daughter win the soccer game.
No problem.
Kid, hand me one of those **subjects!**
PERIOD
What's a subject?
PERIOD
Don't they teach you kids anything in school?
The subject of the sentence is who, where, or what the sentence is about.
HORSES
EVERYBODY
CLEVELAND
THE GIRL
A FOX
THE GIRL
This one should do!
What is the subject of the sentence THE CAR DROVE DOWN THE STREET? See page 40 for the answer.

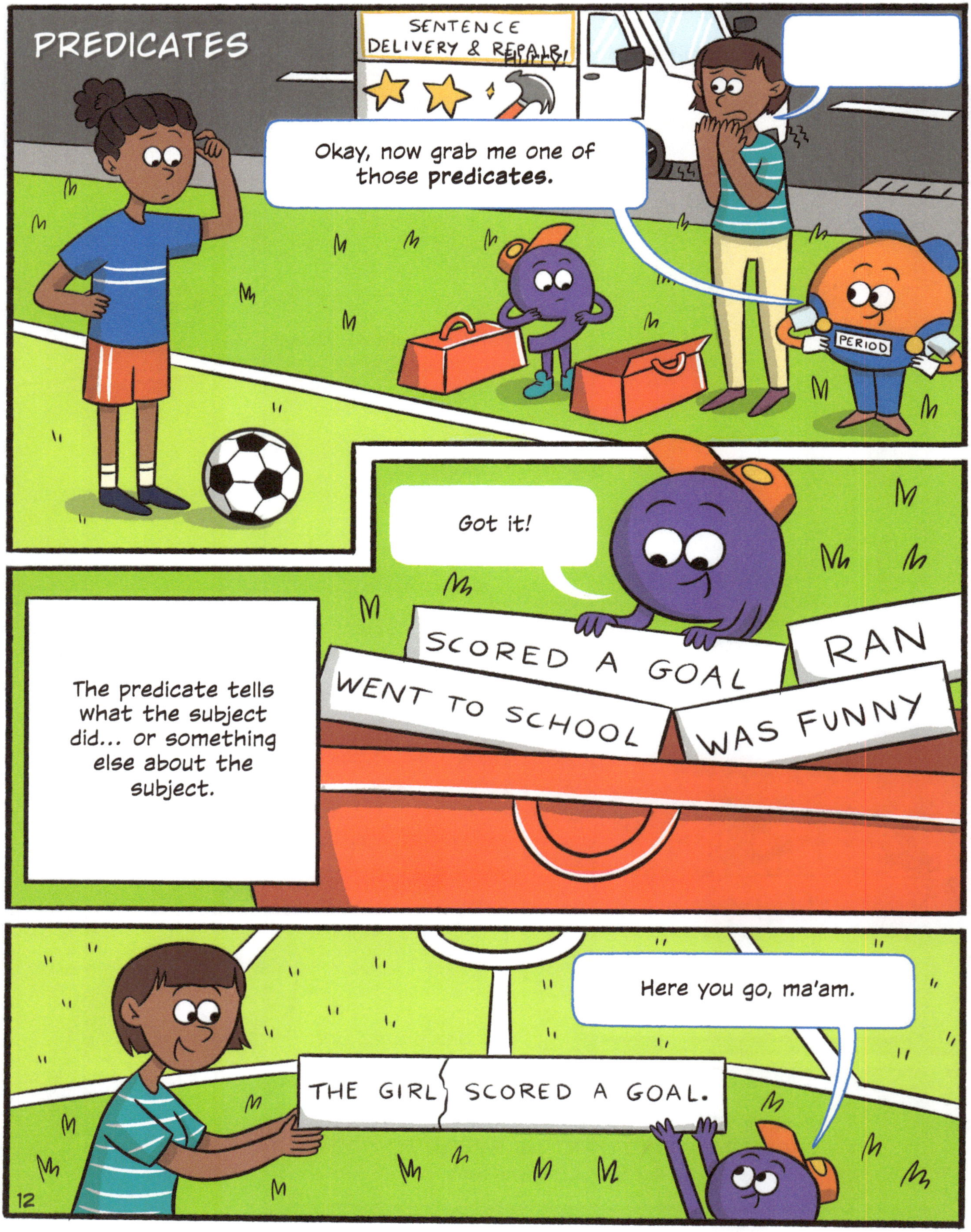
PREDICATES
SENTENCE DELIVERY & REPAIR
Hurry!
Okay, now grab me one of those **predicates**.
PERIOD
Got it!
SCORED A GOAL
RAN
WENT TO SCHOOL
WAS FUNNY
The predicate tells what the subject did... or something else about the subject.
Here you go, ma'am.
THE GIRL SCORED A GOAL.

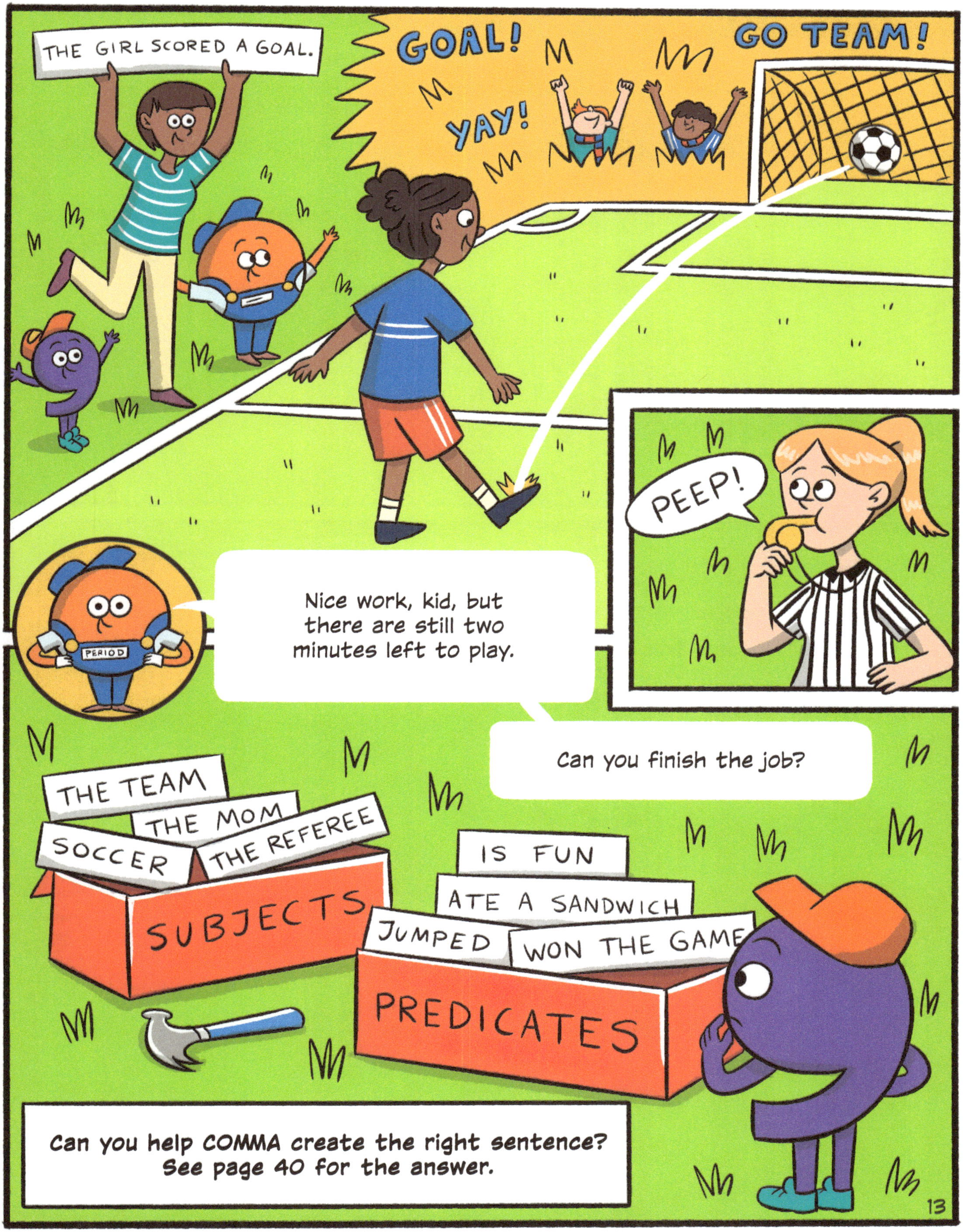
THE GIRL SCORED A GOAL.
GOAL!
YAY!
GO TEAM!
PEEP!
PERIOD
Nice work, kid, but there are still two minutes left to play.
Can you finish the job?
THE TEAM
THE MOM
SOCCER
THE REFEREE
SUBJECTS
IS FUN
ATE A SANDWICH
JUMPED
WON THE GAME
PREDICATES
Can you help COMMA create the right sentence?
See page 40 for the answer.

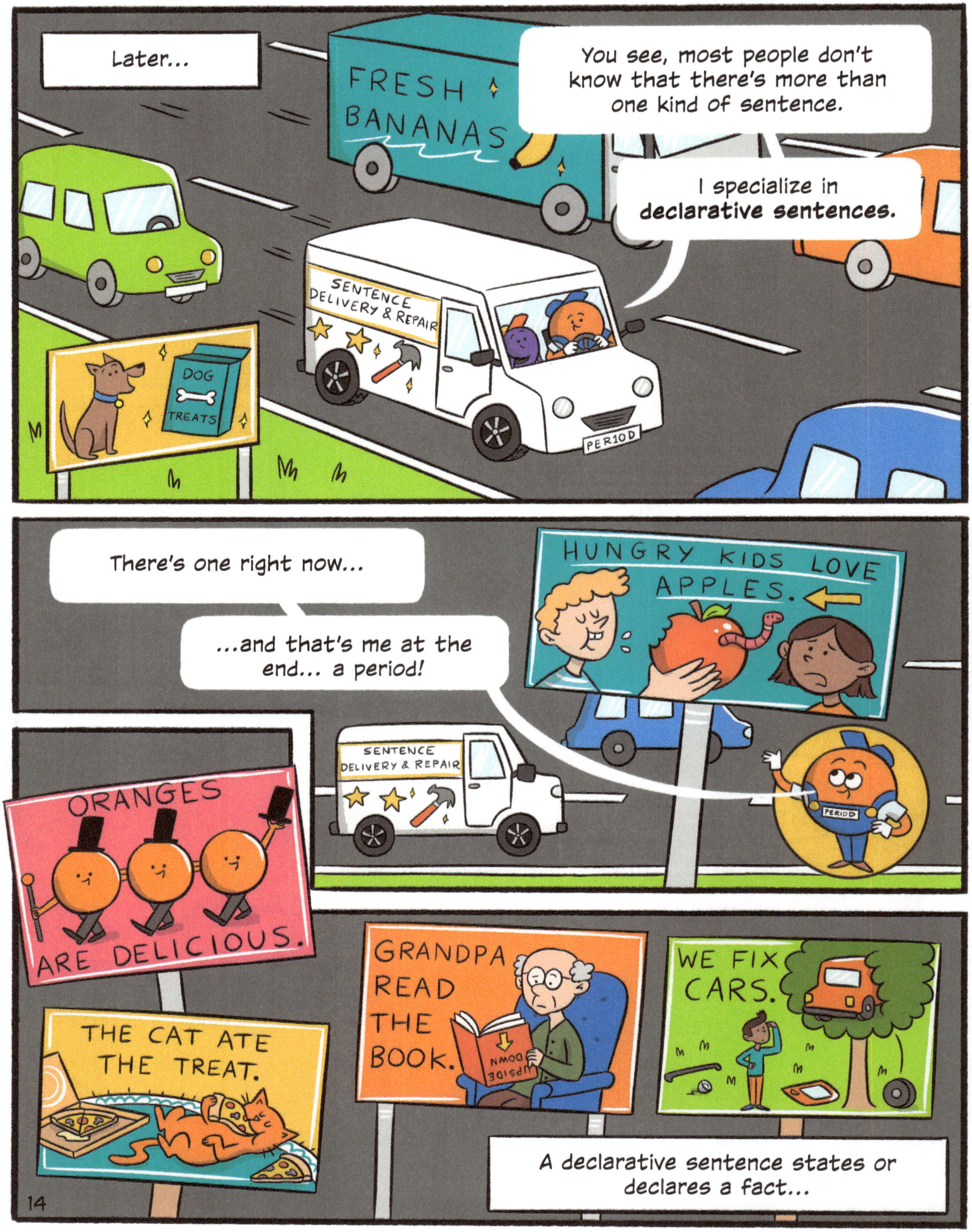

Later...
FRESH BANANAS
You see, most people don't know that there's more than one kind of sentence.
I specialize in **declarative sentences.**
SENTENCE DELIVERY & REPAIR
PERIOD
DOG TREATS
There's one right now...
...and that's me at the end... a period!
HUNGRY KIDS LOVE APPLES.
SENTENCE DELIVERY & REPAIR
PERIOD
ORANGES ARE DELICIOUS.
THE CAT ATE THE TREAT.
GRANDPA READ THE BOOK.
UPSIDE DOWN
WE FIX CARS.
A declarative sentence states or declares a fact...

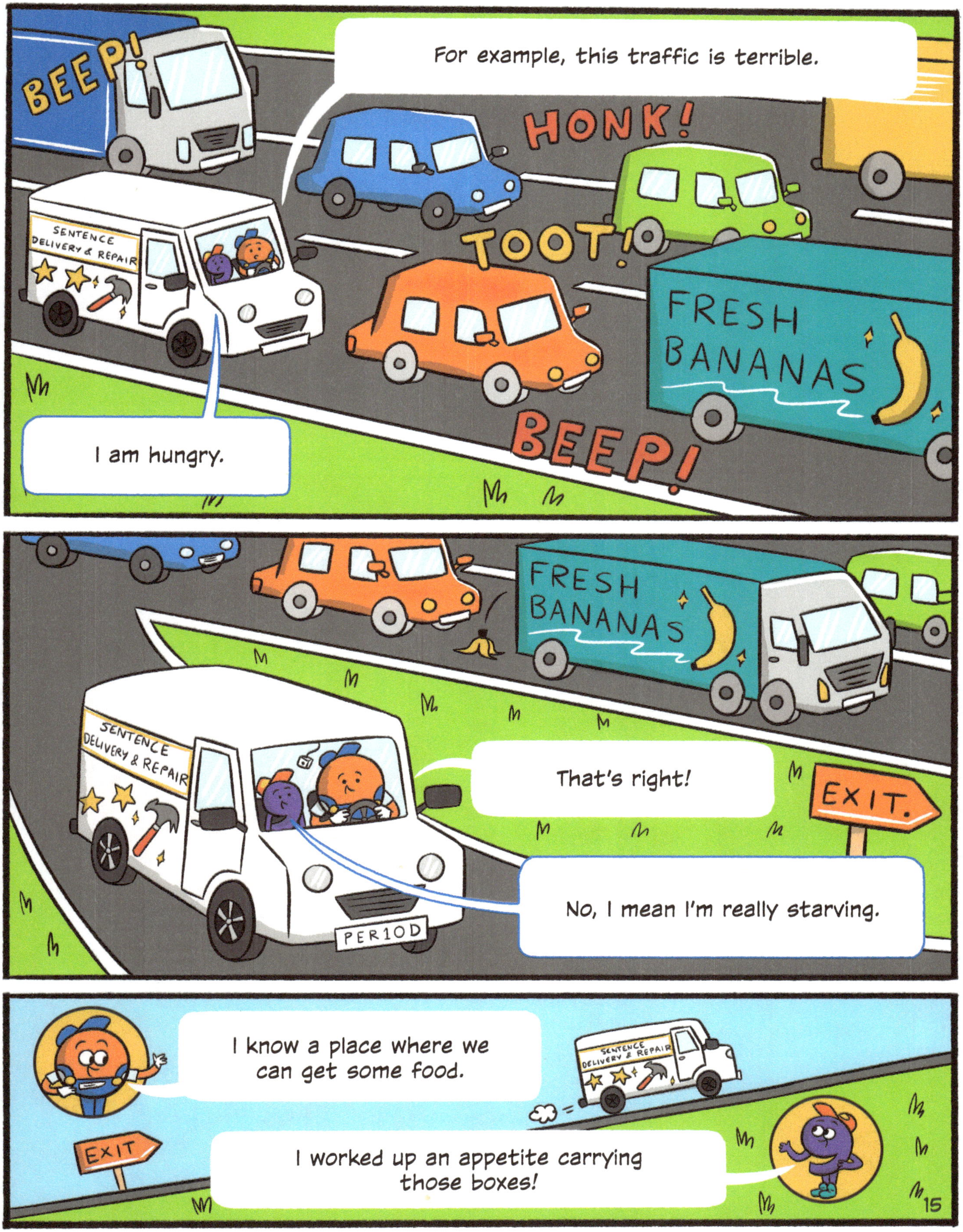
BEEP!
For example, this traffic is terrible.
HONK!
SENTENCE DELIVERY & REPAIR
TOOT!
FRESH BANANAS
I am hungry.
BEEP!
FRESH BANANAS
SENTENCE DELIVERY & REPAIR
That's right!
EXIT
PERIOD
No, I mean I'm really starving.
I know a place where we can get some food.
SENTENCE DELIVERY & REPAIR
EXIT
I worked up an appetite carrying those boxes!

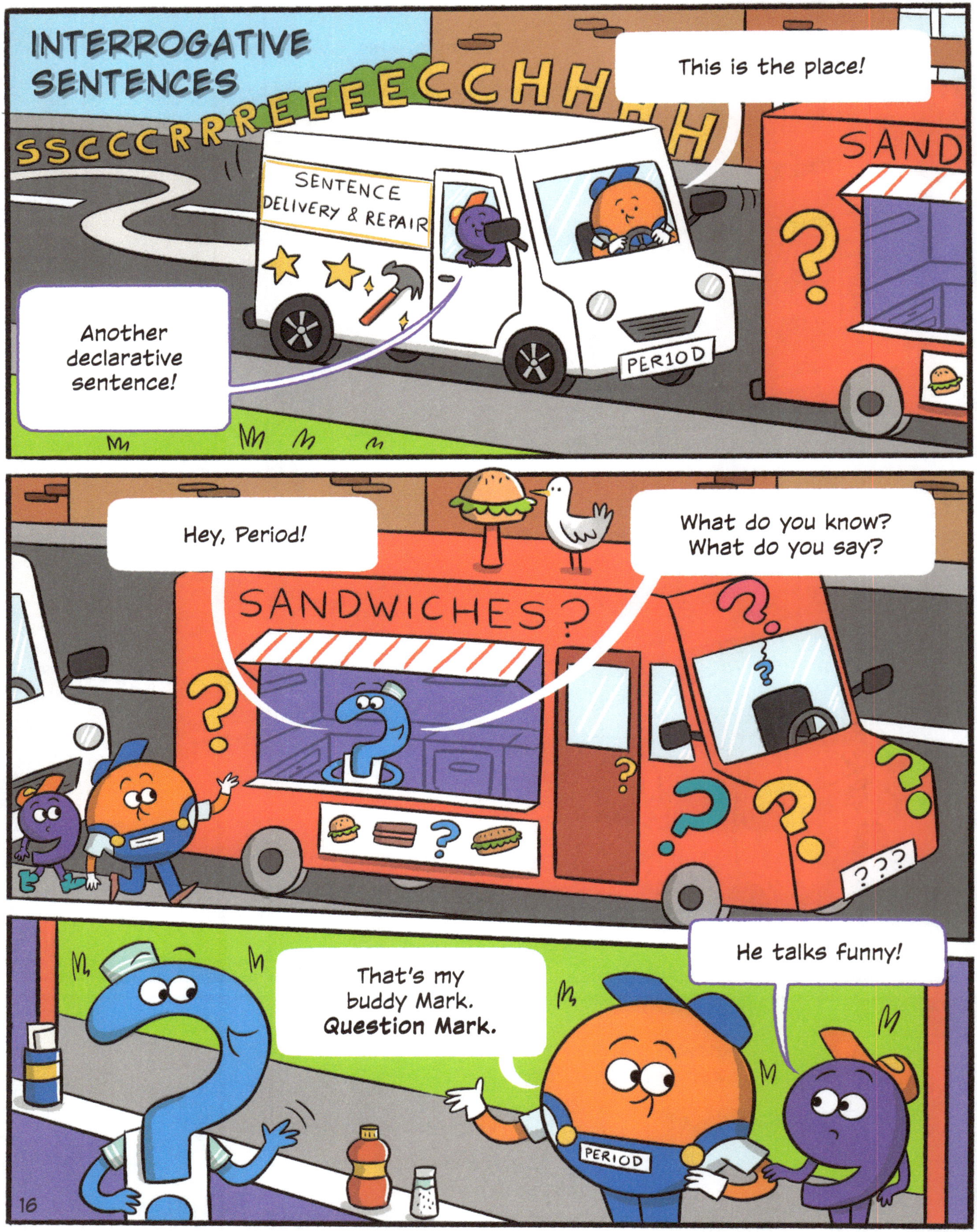
INTERROGATIVE SENTENCES
SSCCCRRREEEEECCHHHHH
This is the place!
SENTENCE DELIVERY & REPAIR
PERIOD
Another declarative sentence!
SAND
Hey, Period!
What do you know? What do you say?
SANDWICHES?
???
That's my buddy Mark. **Question Mark.**
He talks funny!
PERIOD

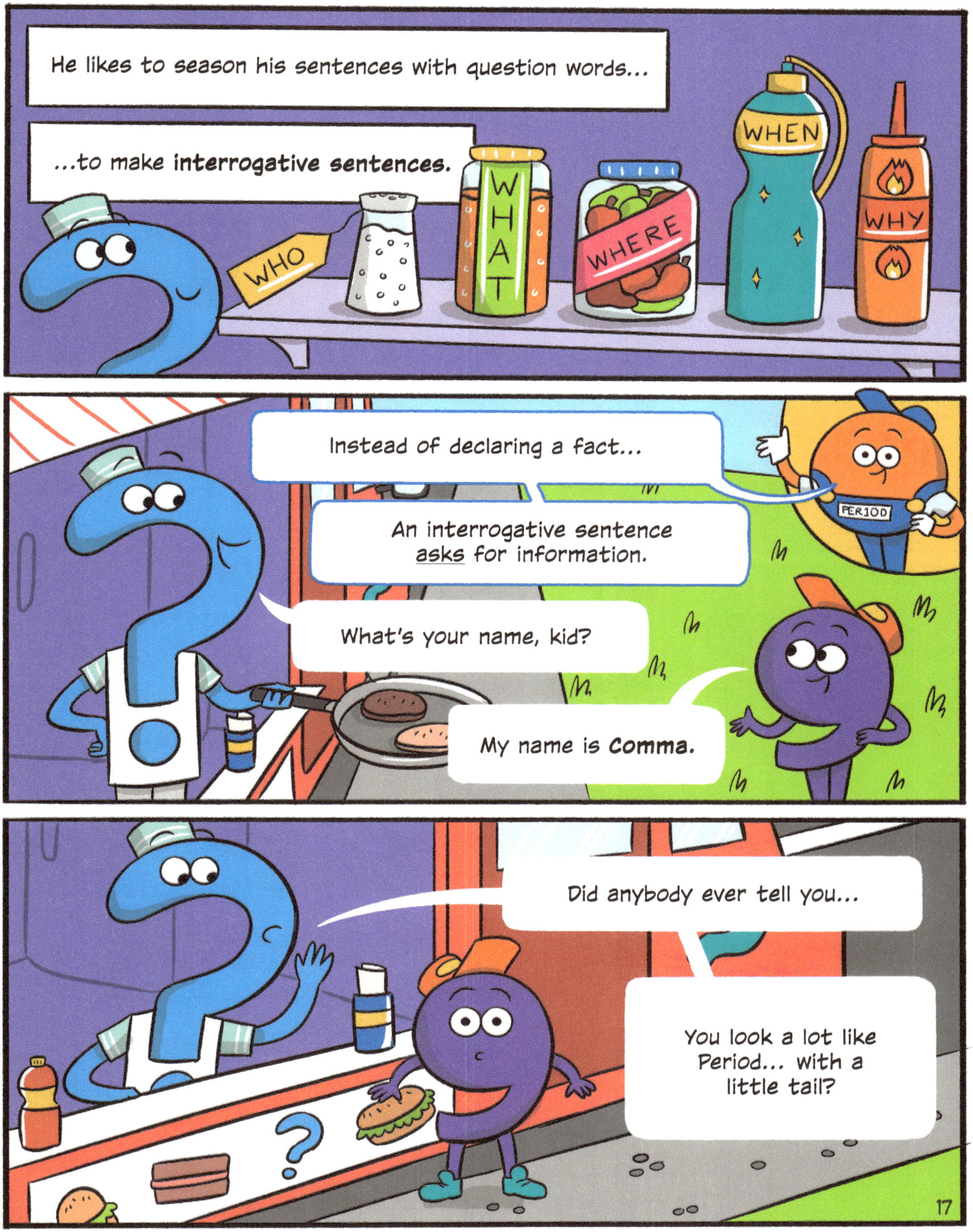
He likes to season his sentences with question words...
...to make **interrogative sentences.**
WHO
WHAT
WHERE
WHEN
WHY
Instead of declaring a fact...
An interrogative sentence asks for information.
PERIOD
What's your name, kid?
My name is **Comma.**
Did anybody ever tell you...
You look a lot like Period... with a little tail?

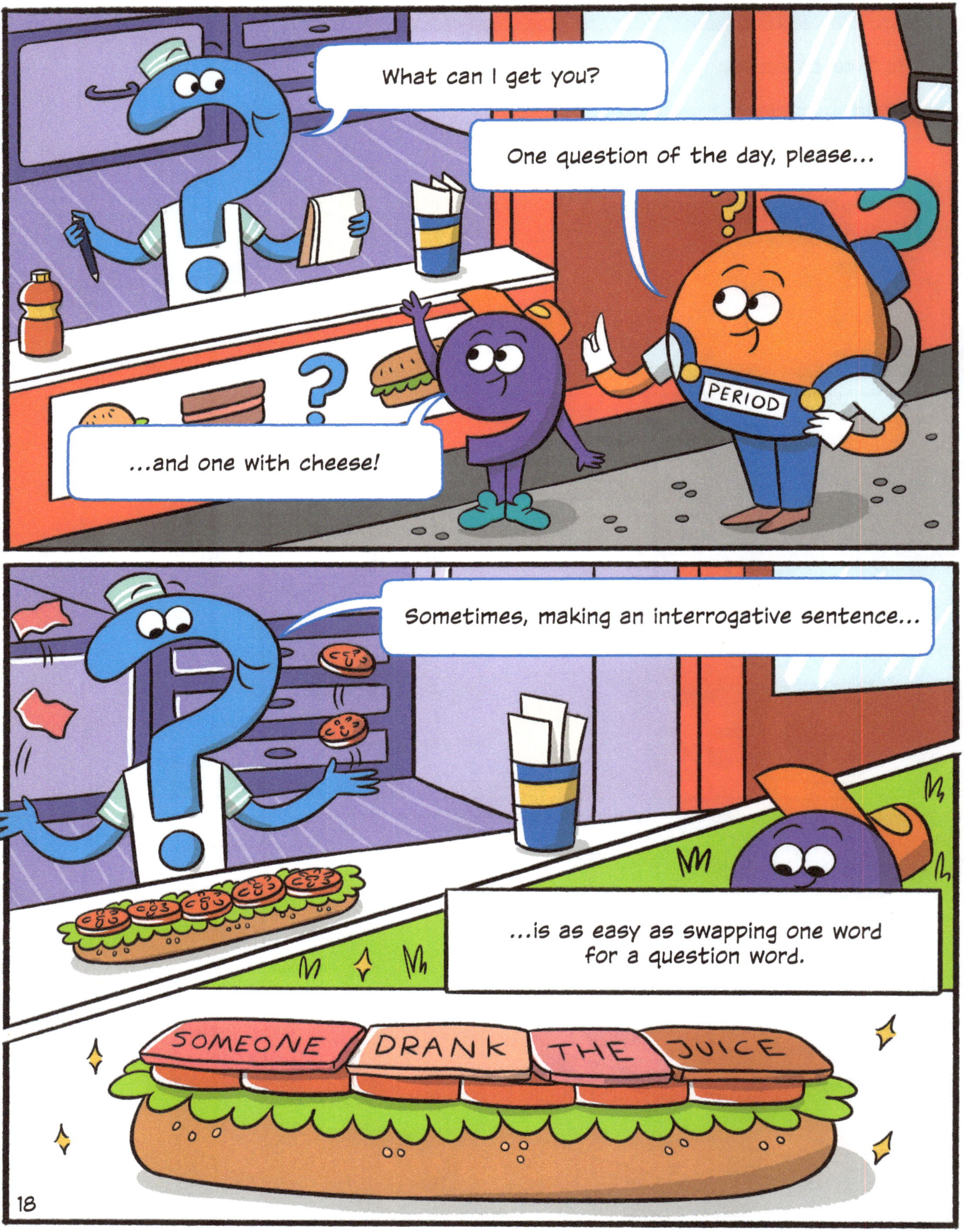
What can I get you?
One question of the day, please...
...and one with cheese!
PERIOD
Sometimes, making an interrogative sentence...
...is as easy as swapping one word for a question word.
SOMEONE DRANK THE JUICE

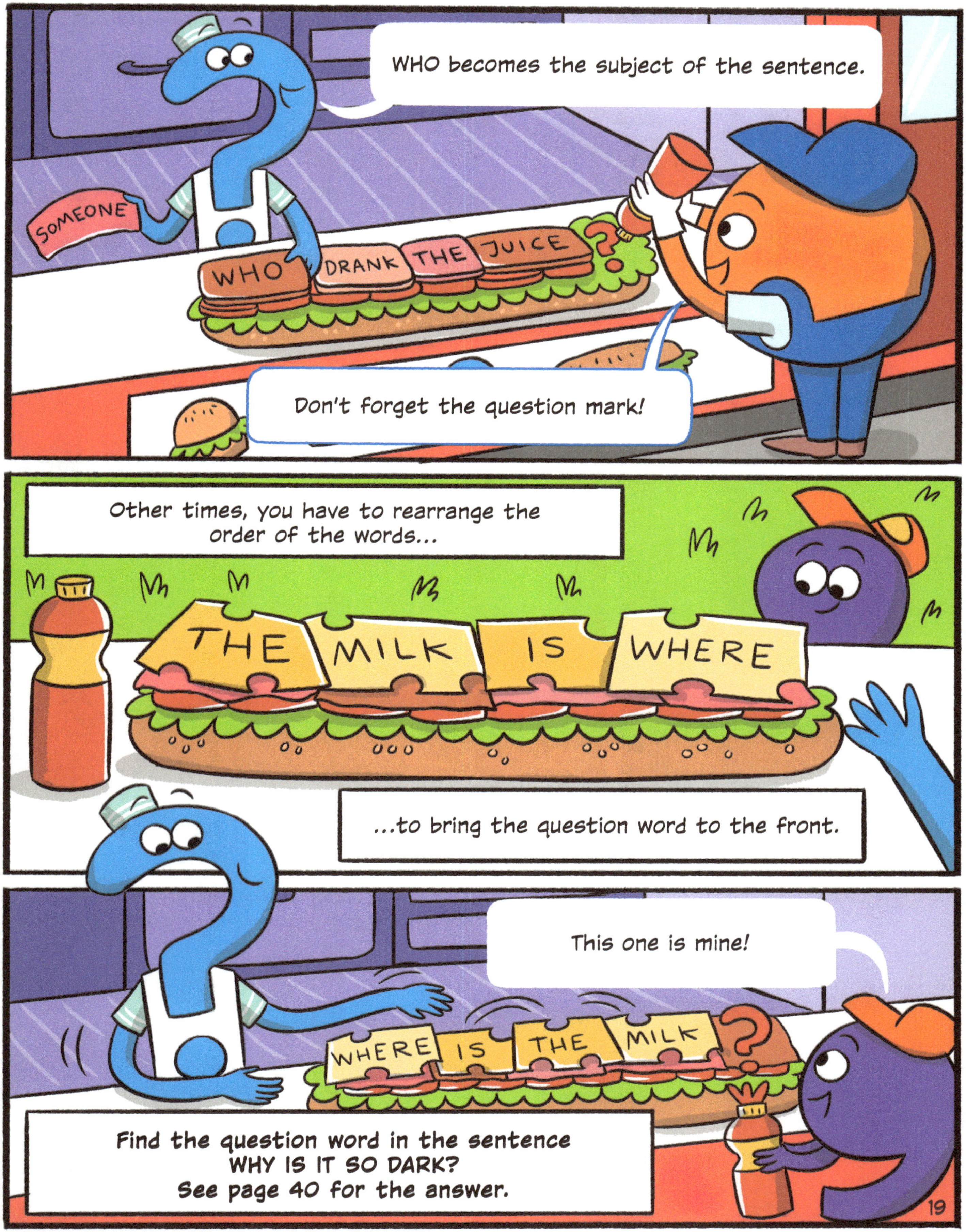
WHO becomes the subject of the sentence.
SOMEONE
WHO DRANK THE JUICE ?
Don't forget the question mark!
Other times, you have to rearrange the order of the words...
THE MILK IS WHERE
...to bring the question word to the front.
This one is mine!
WHERE IS THE MILK ?
Find the question word in the sentence
WHY IS IT SO DARK?
See page 40 for the answer.

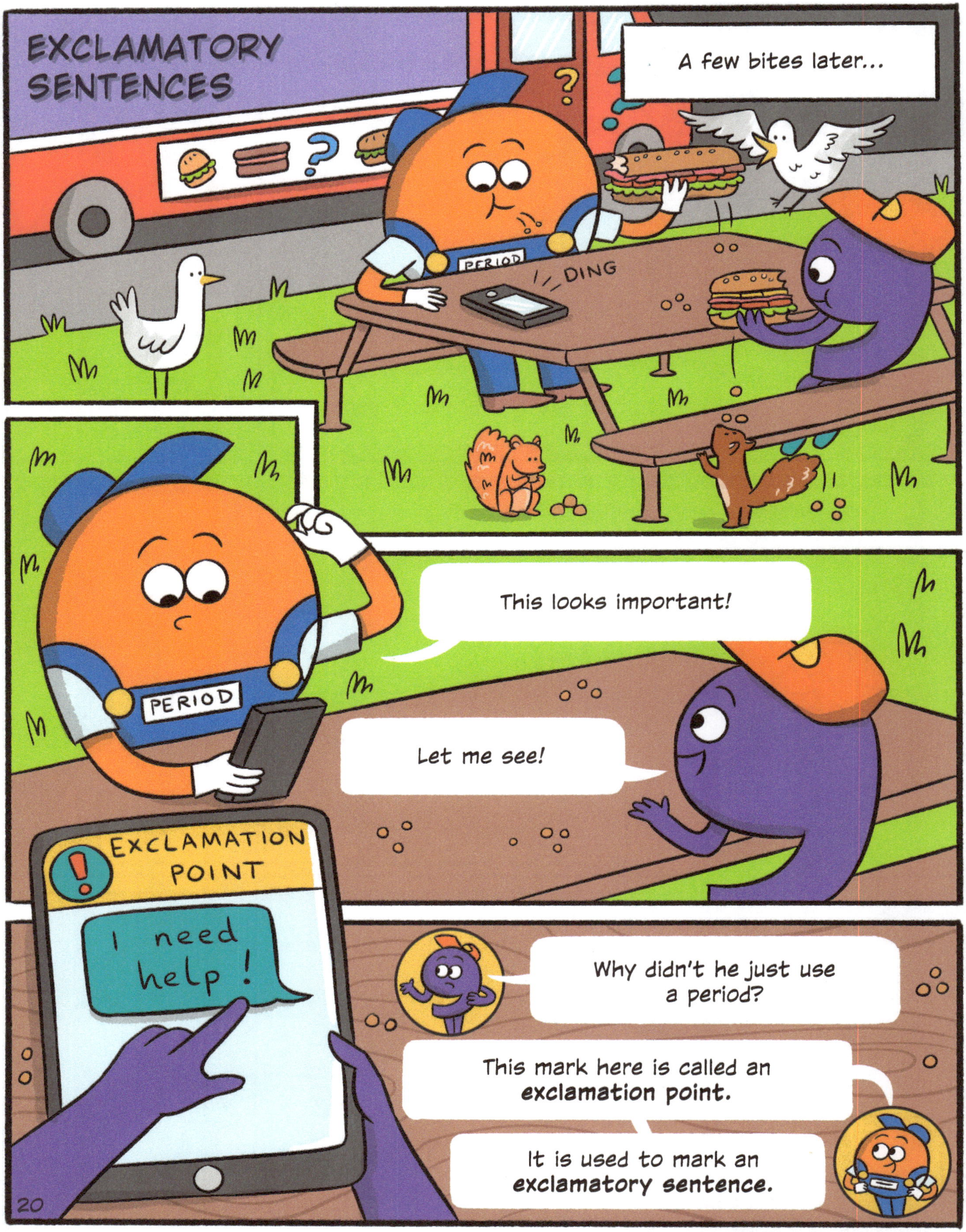
EXCLAMATORY SENTENCES
A few bites later...
DING
PERIOD
This looks important!
Let me see!
EXCLAMATION POINT
I need help!
Why didn't he just use a period?
This mark here is called an **exclamation point.**
It is used to mark an **exclamatory sentence.**

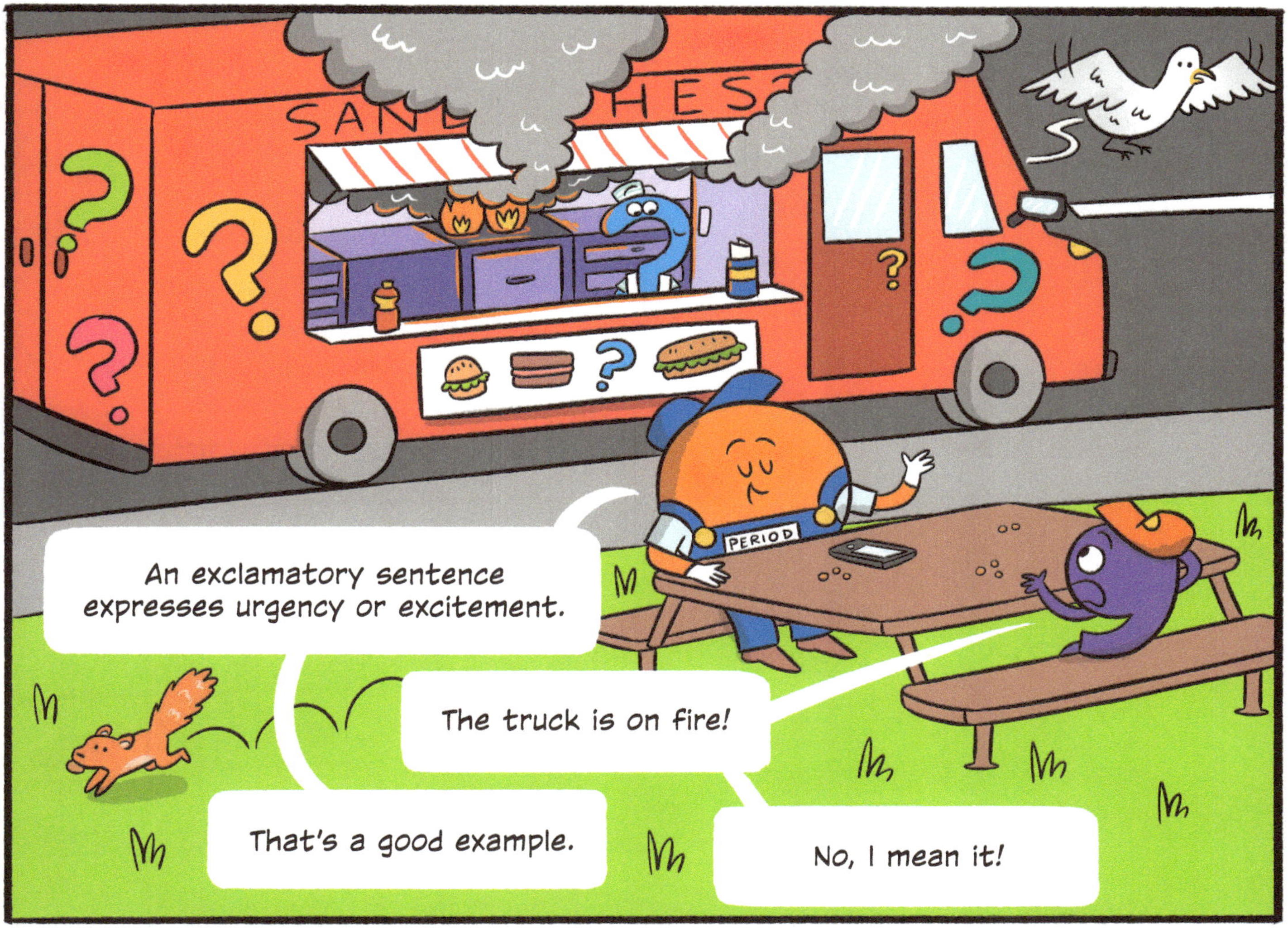
SANDWICHES
An exclamatory sentence expresses urgency or excitement.
The truck is on fire!
That's a good example.
No, I mean it!
PERIOD

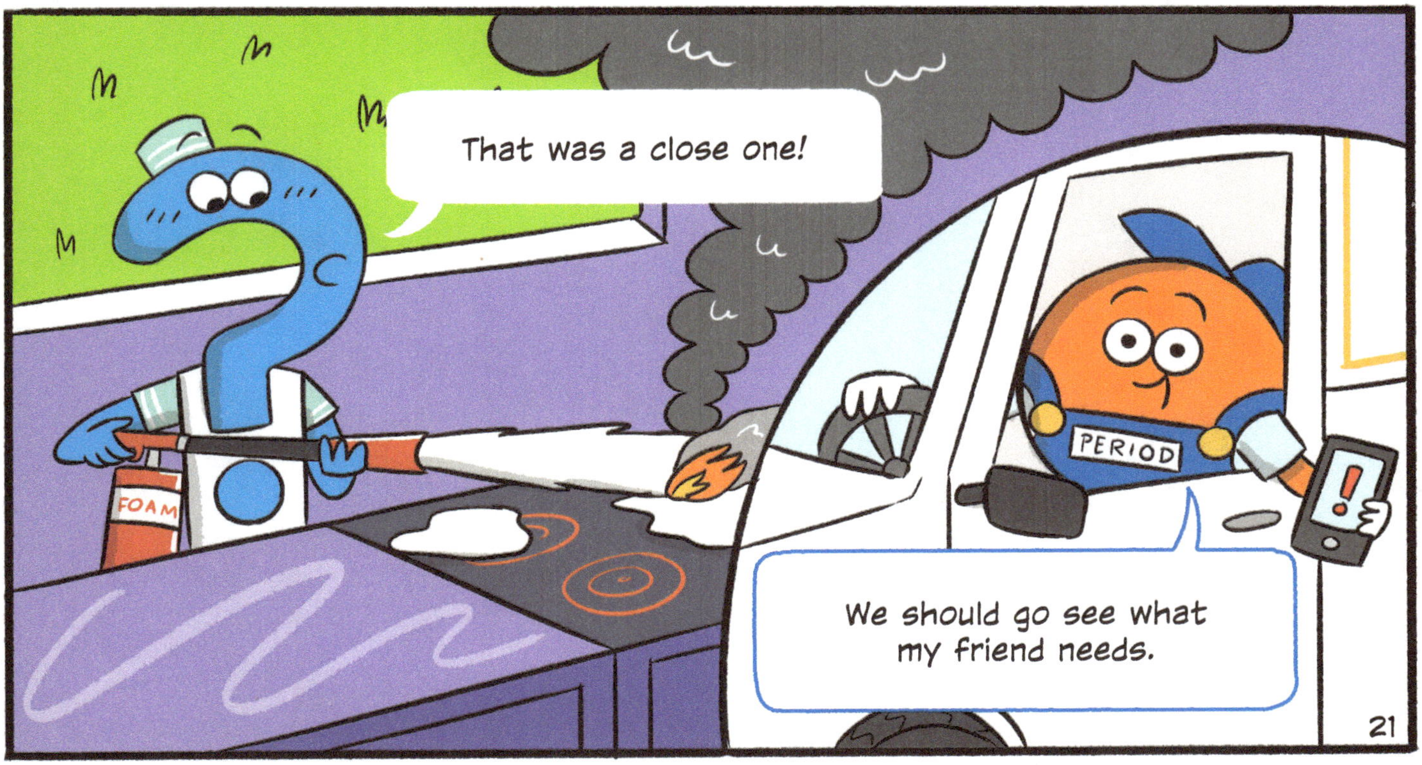
That was a close one!
FOAM
PERIOD
We should go see what my friend needs.

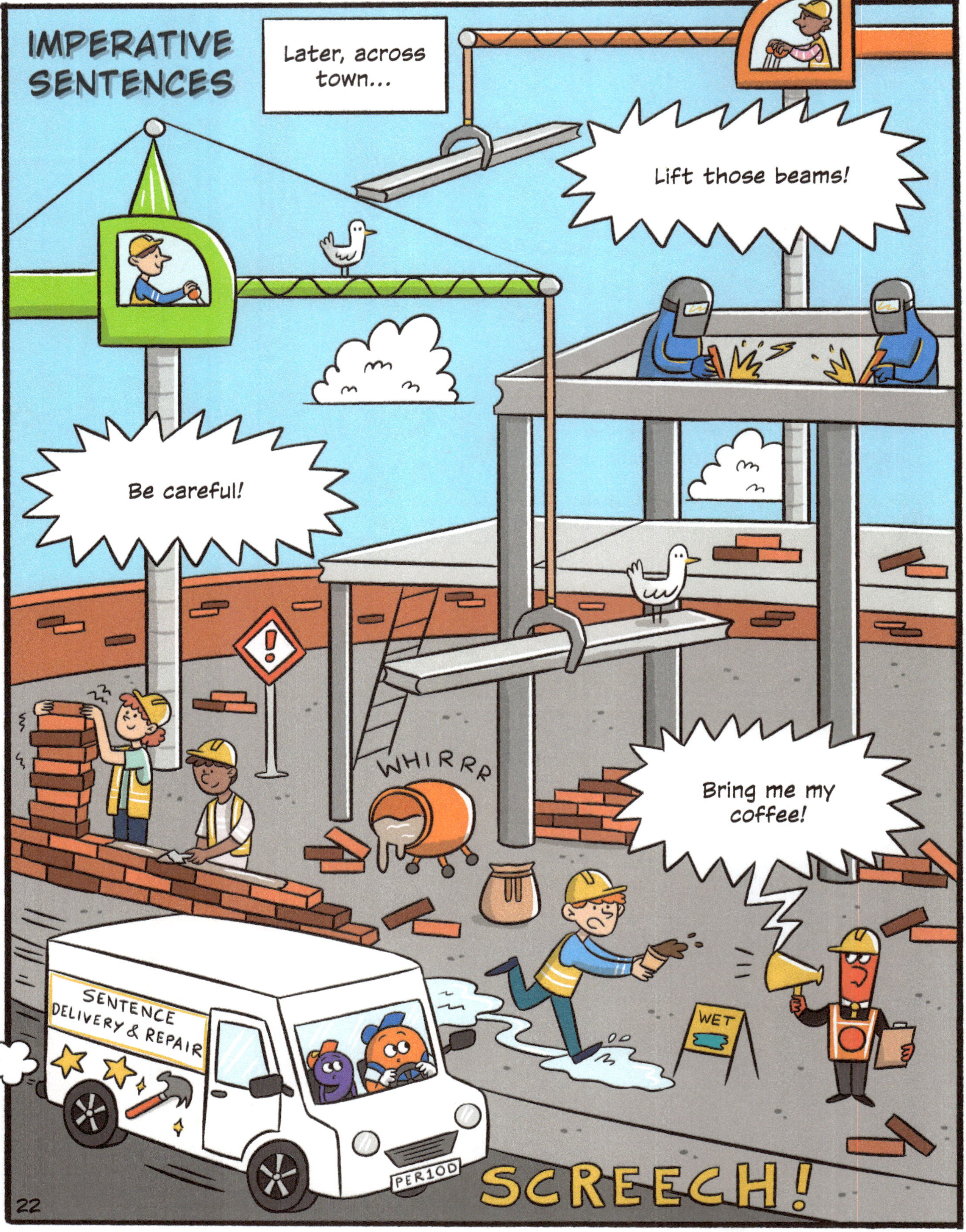
IMPERATIVE SENTENCES
Later, across town...
Lift those beams!
Be careful!
WHIRRR
Bring me my coffee!
SENTENCE DELIVERY & REPAIR
WET
PER1OD
SCREECH!

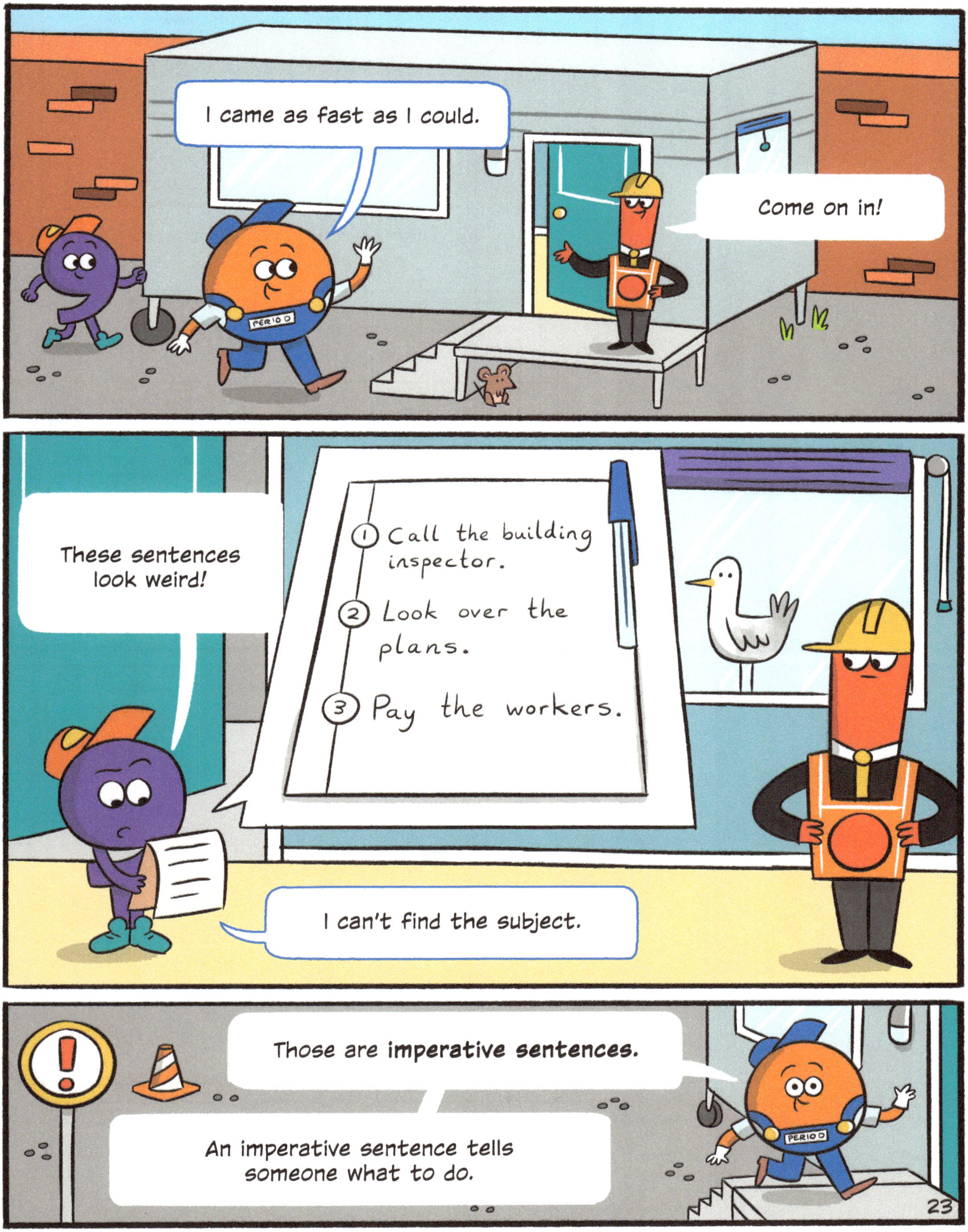
I came as fast as I could.
Come on in!
PERIOD
These sentences look weird!
1 Call the building inspector.
2 Look over the plans.
3 Pay the workers.
I can't find the subject.
Those are **imperative sentences.**
An imperative sentence tells someone what to do.
PERIOD

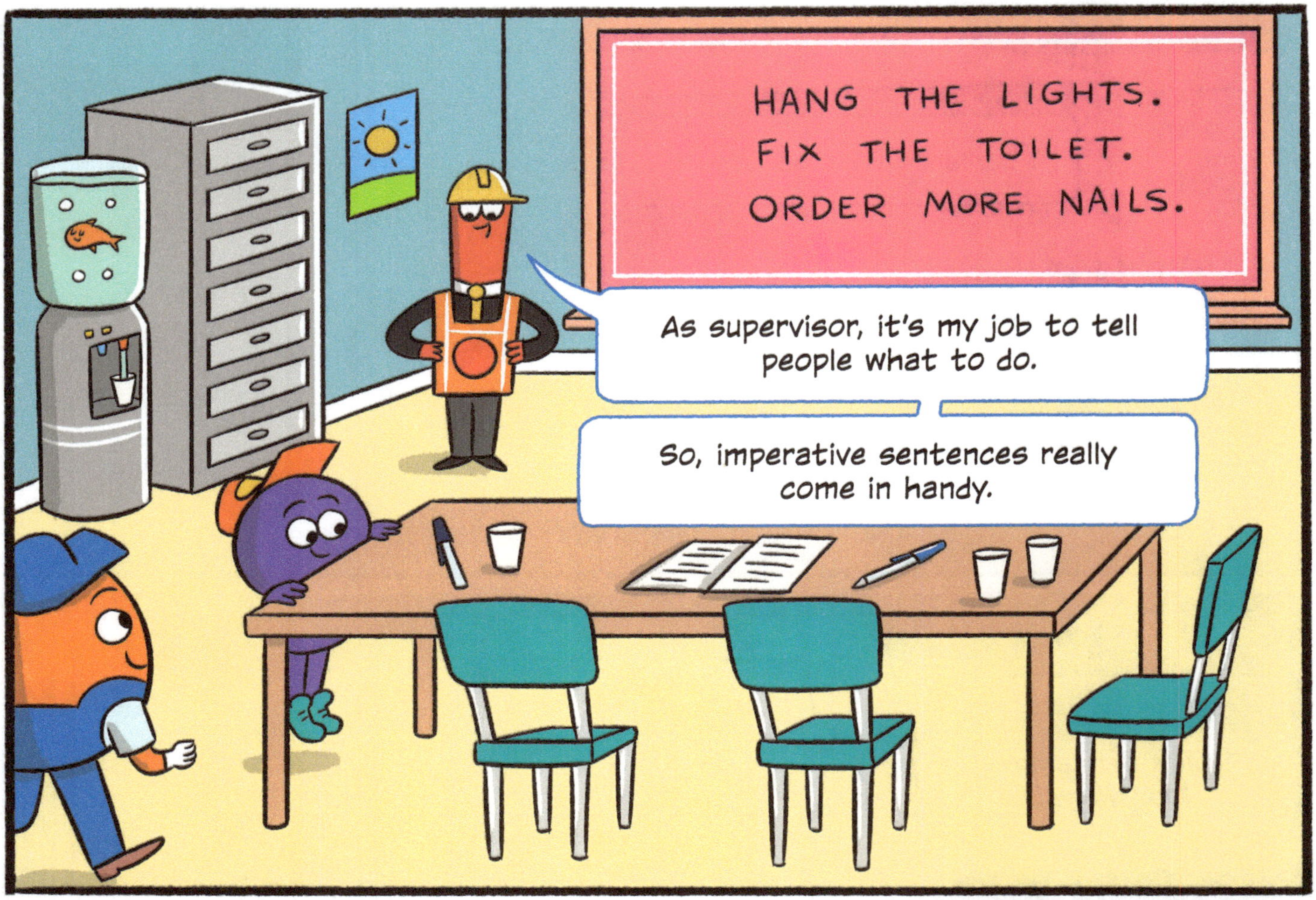
HANG THE LIGHTS.
FIX THE TOILET.
ORDER MORE NAILS.
As supervisor, it's my job to tell people what to do.
So, imperative sentences really come in handy.

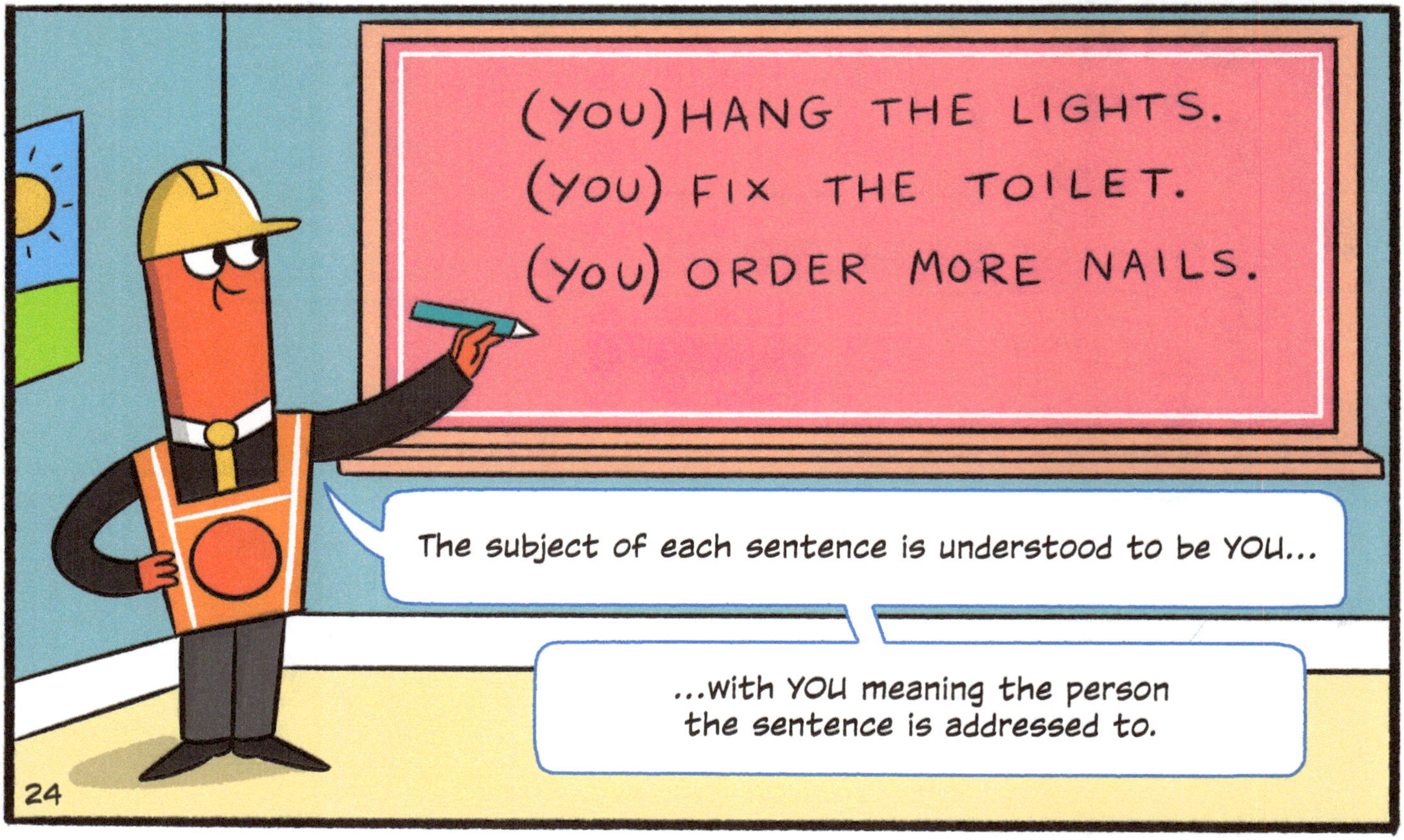
(YOU) HANG THE LIGHTS.
(YOU) FIX THE TOILET.
(YOU) ORDER MORE NAILS.
The subject of each sentence is understood to be YOU...
...with YOU meaning the person the sentence is addressed to.

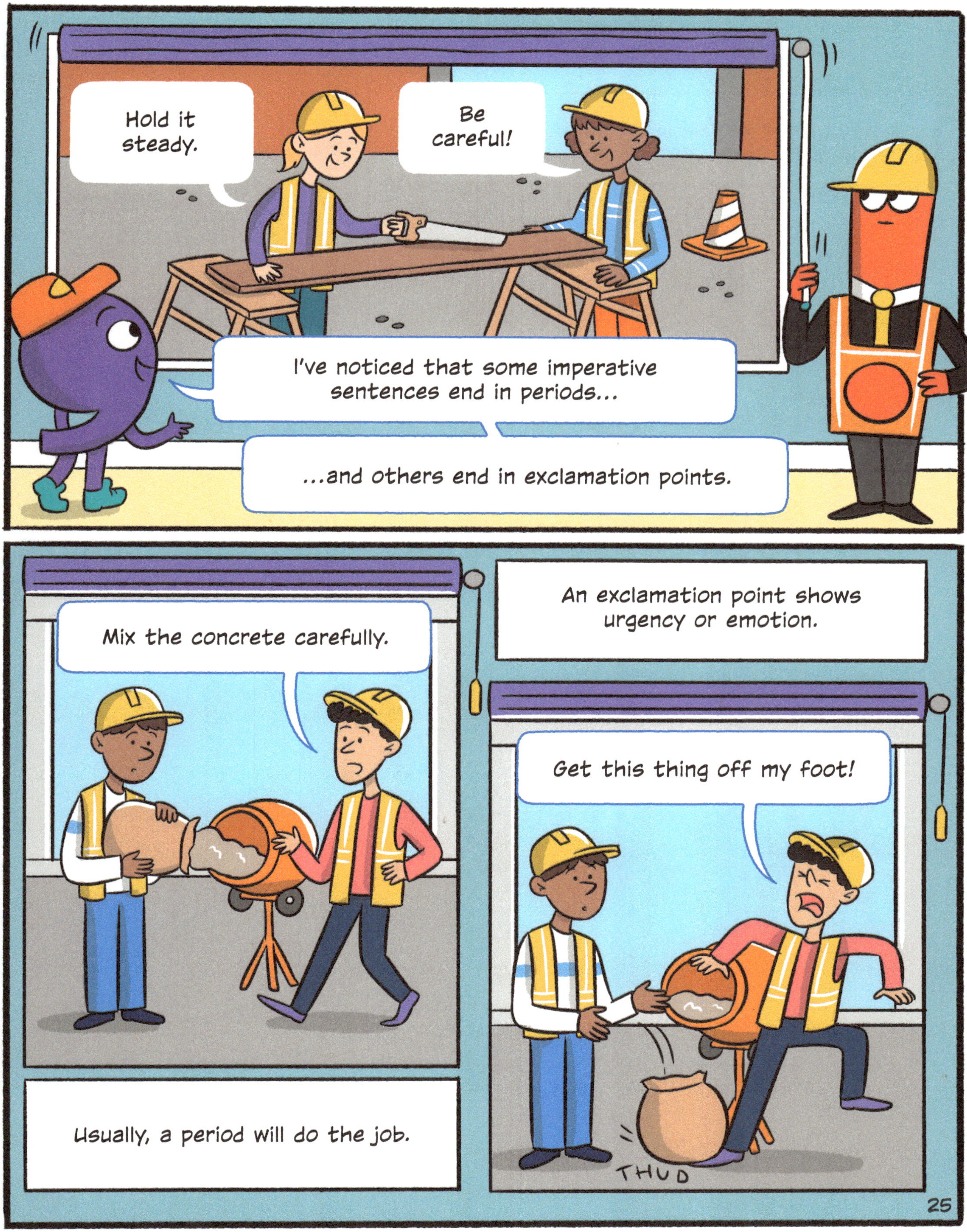
Hold it steady.
Be careful!
I've noticed that some imperative sentences end in periods...
...and others end in exclamation points.
Mix the concrete carefully.
Usually, a period will do the job.
An exclamation point shows urgency or emotion.
Get this thing off my foot!
THUD

SORT THE SENTENCES

A huge shipment of sentences has arrived! Help sort them into their proper types.

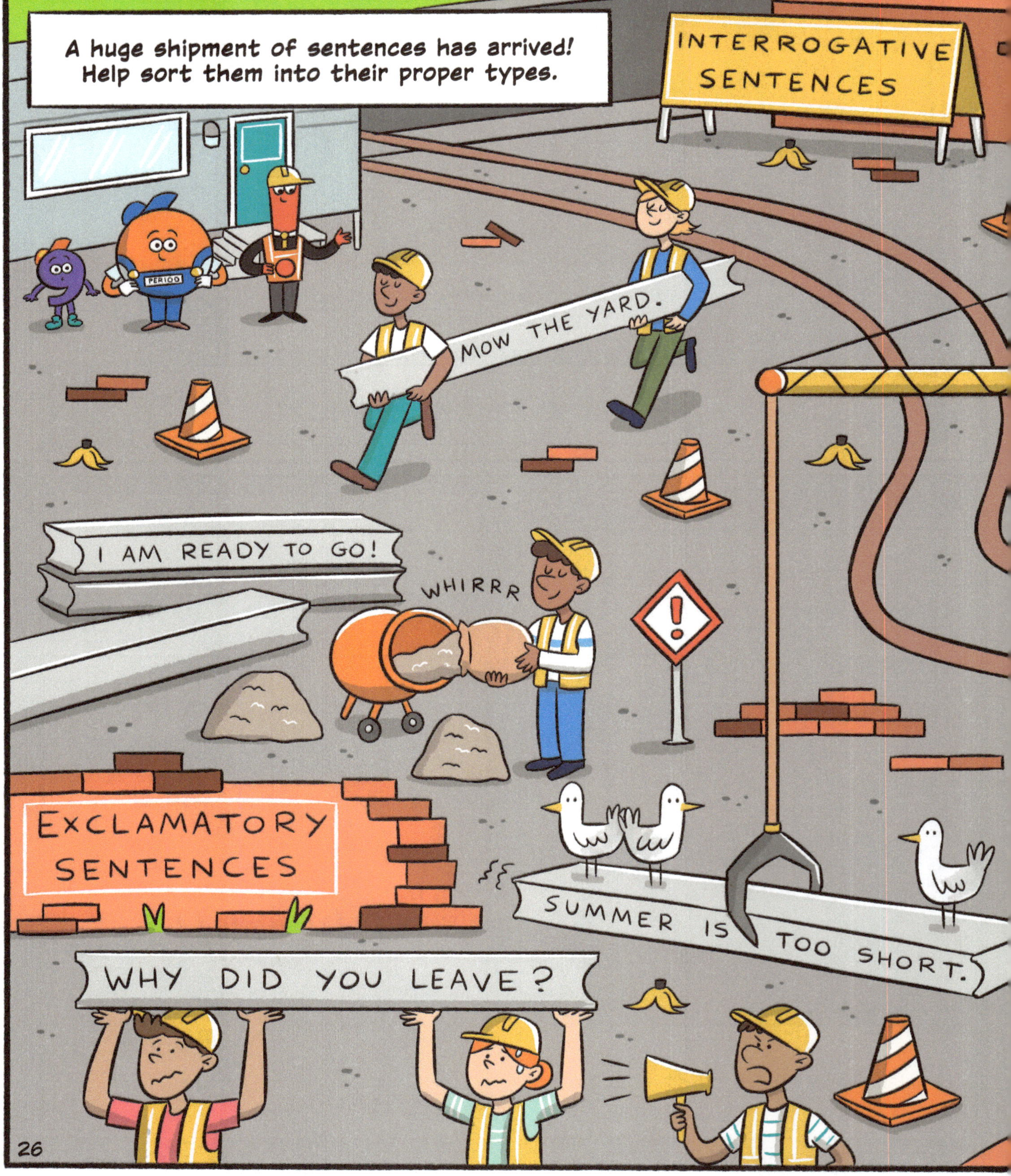
INTERROGATIVE SENTENCES
PERIOD
MOW THE YARD.
I AM READY TO GO!
WHIRRR
EXCLAMATORY SENTENCES
SUMMER IS TOO SHORT.
WHY DID YOU LEAVE?

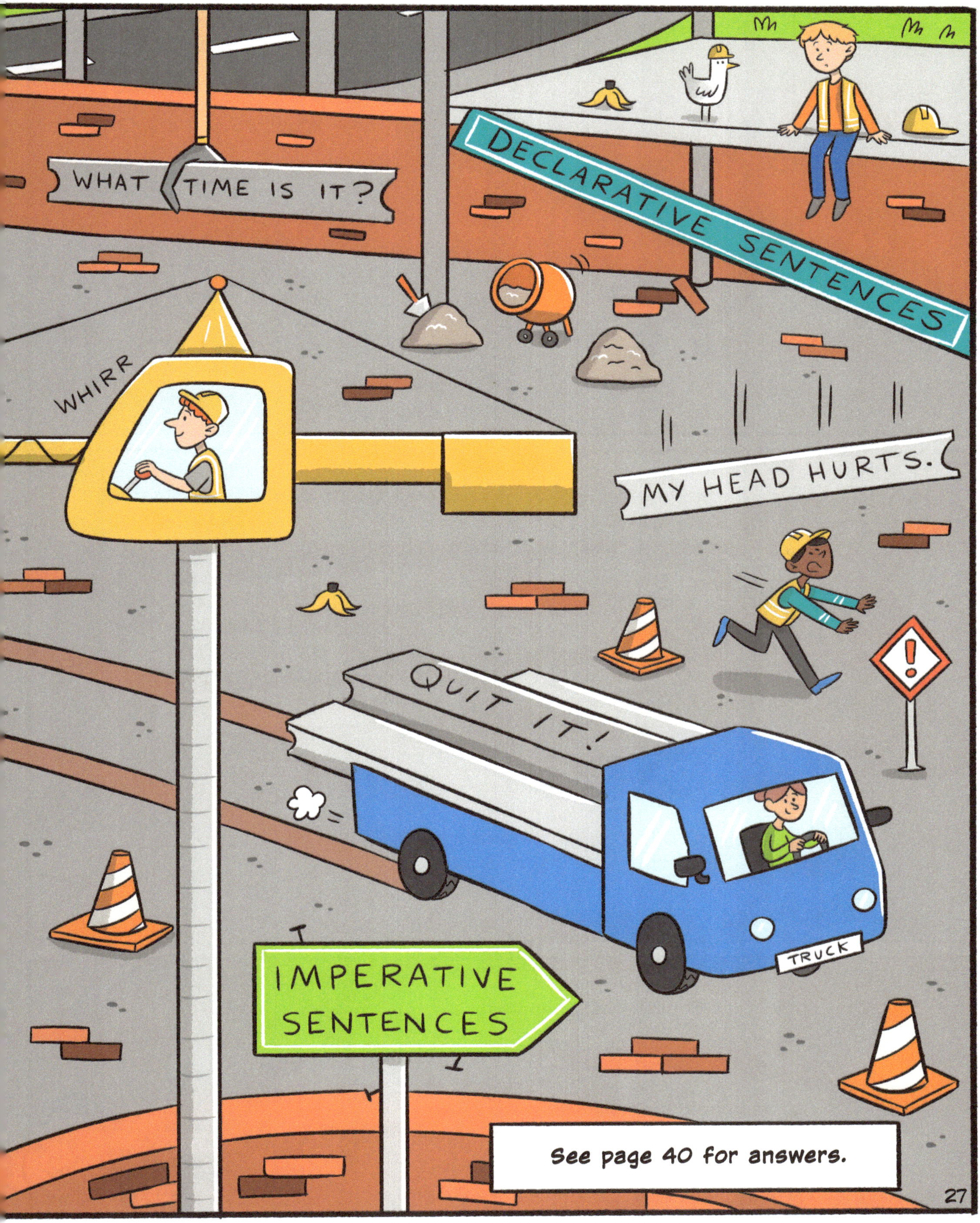
WHAT TIME IS IT?
DECLARATIVE SENTENCES
WHIRR
MY HEAD HURTS.
QUIT IT!
TRUCK
IMPERATIVE SENTENCES

See page 40 for answers.

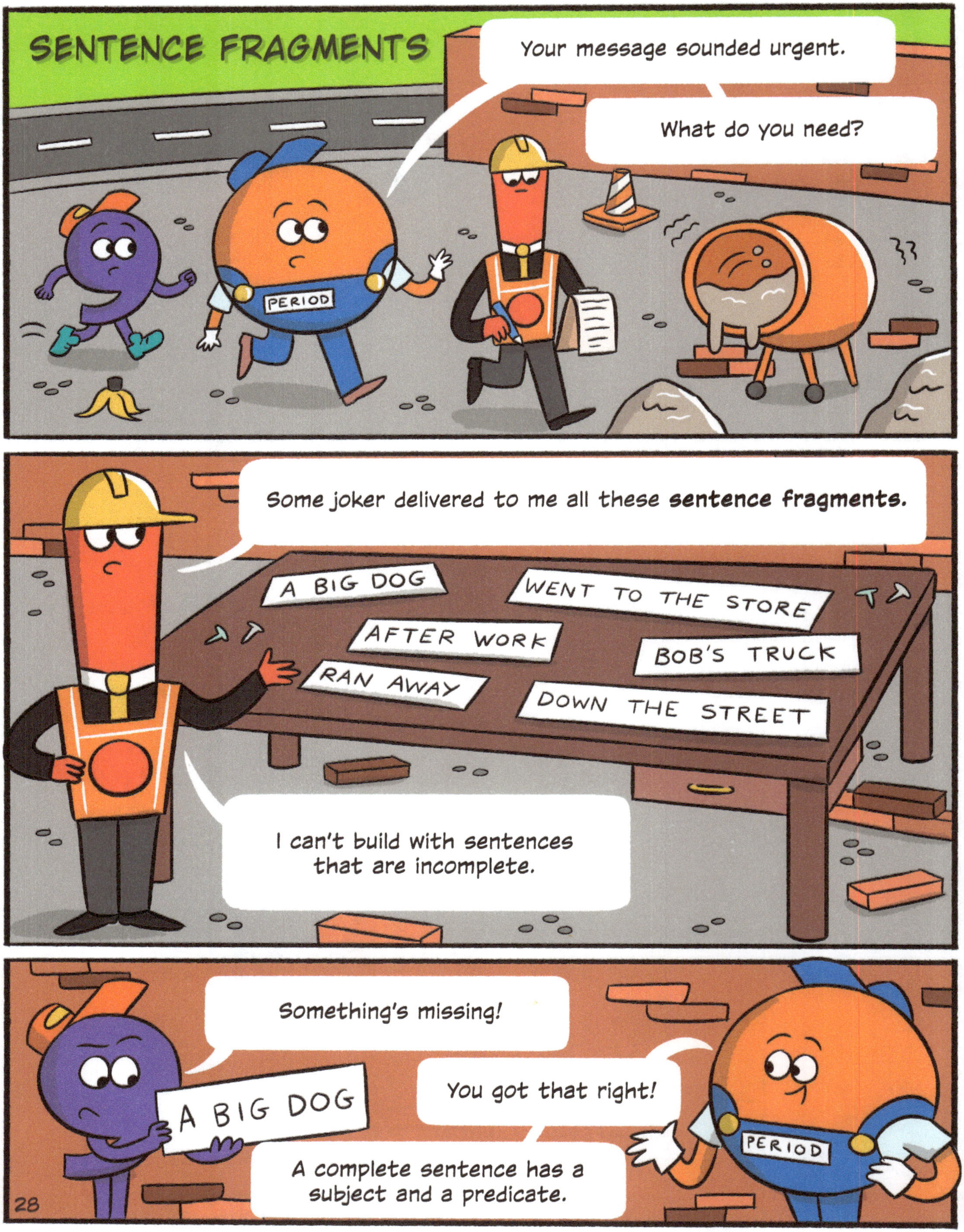
SENTENCE FRAGMENTS
Your message sounded urgent.
What do you need?
PERIOD
Some joker delivered to me all these **sentence fragments.**
A BIG DOG
WENT TO THE STORE
AFTER WORK
BOB'S TRUCK
RAN AWAY
DOWN THE STREET
I can't build with sentences that are incomplete.
Something's missing!
A BIG DOG
You got that right!
PERIOD
A complete sentence has a subject and a predicate.

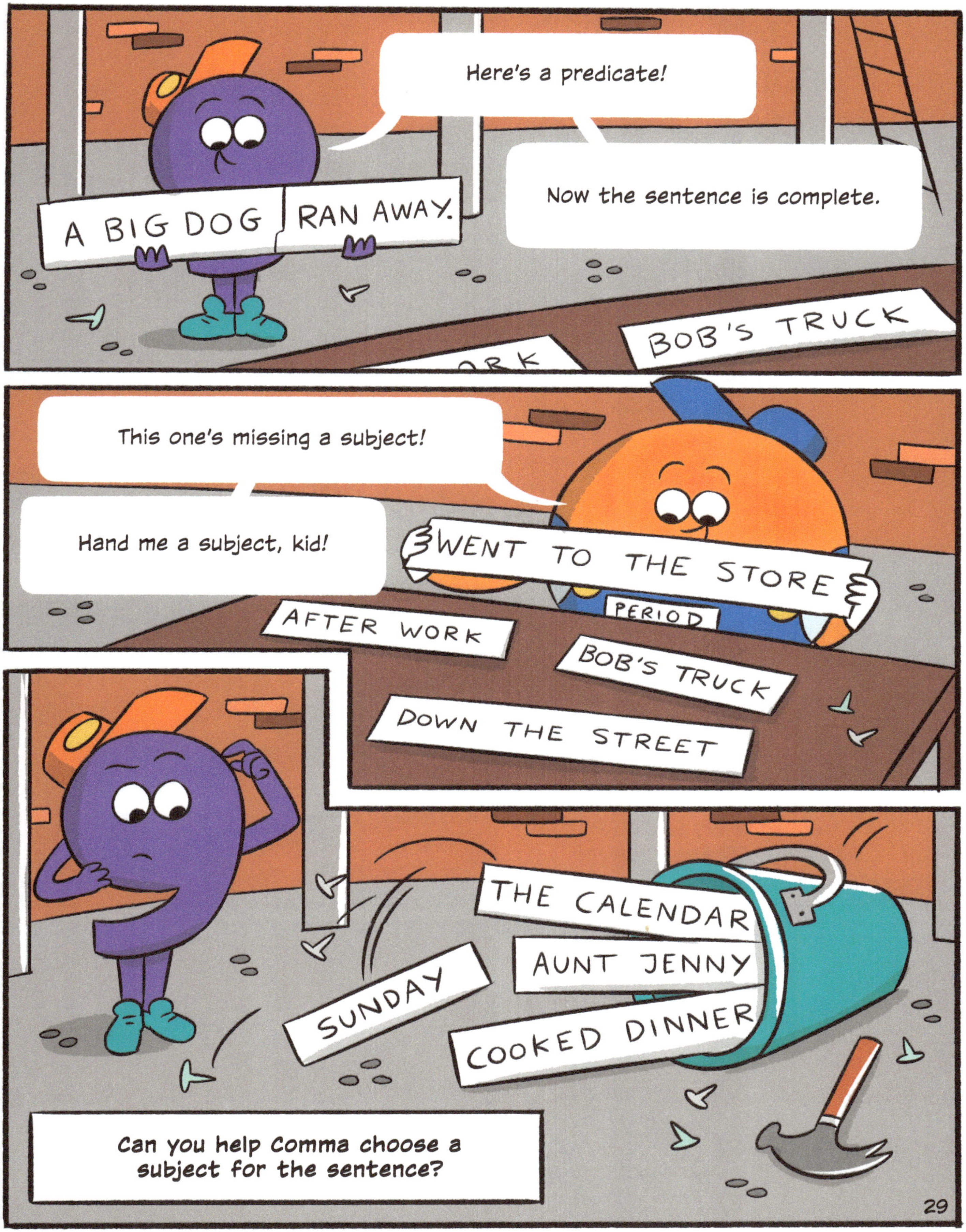

A BIG DOG RAN AWAY.
Here's a predicate!
Now the sentence is complete.
BOB'S TRUCK
This one's missing a subject!
Hand me a subject, kid!
WENT TO THE STORE
PERIOD
AFTER WORK
BOB'S TRUCK
DOWN THE STREET
THE CALENDAR
AUNT JENNY
SUNDAY
COOKED DINNER
Can you help Comma choose a subject for the sentence?

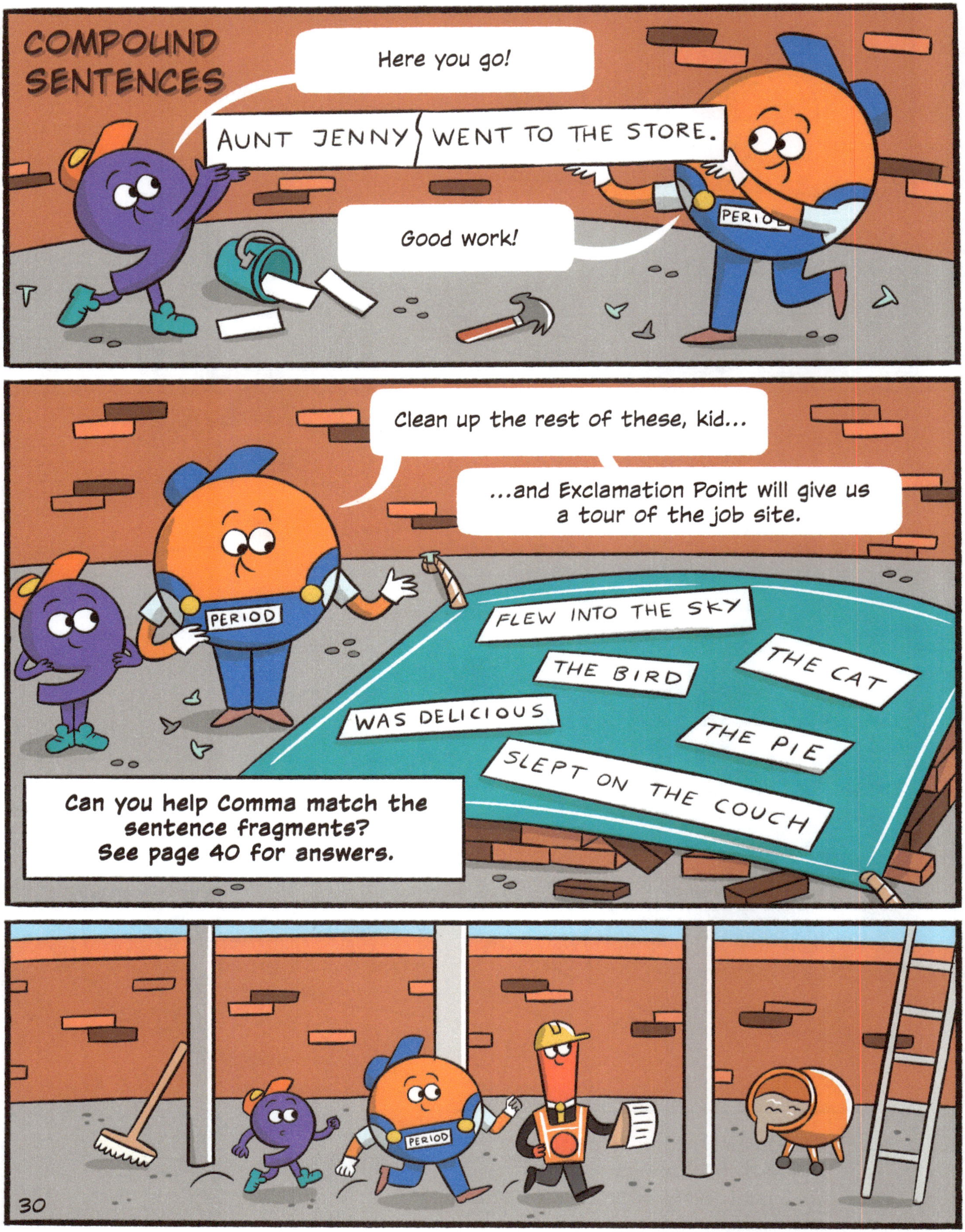
COMPOUND SENTENCES
Here you go!
AUNT JENNY WENT TO THE STORE.
Good work!
PERIOD
Clean up the rest of these, kid...
...and Exclamation Point will give us a tour of the job site.
PERIOD
FLEW INTO THE SKY
THE CAT
THE BIRD
WAS DELICIOUS
THE PIE
SLEPT ON THE COUCH
Can you help Comma match the sentence fragments?
See page 40 for answers.
PERIOD

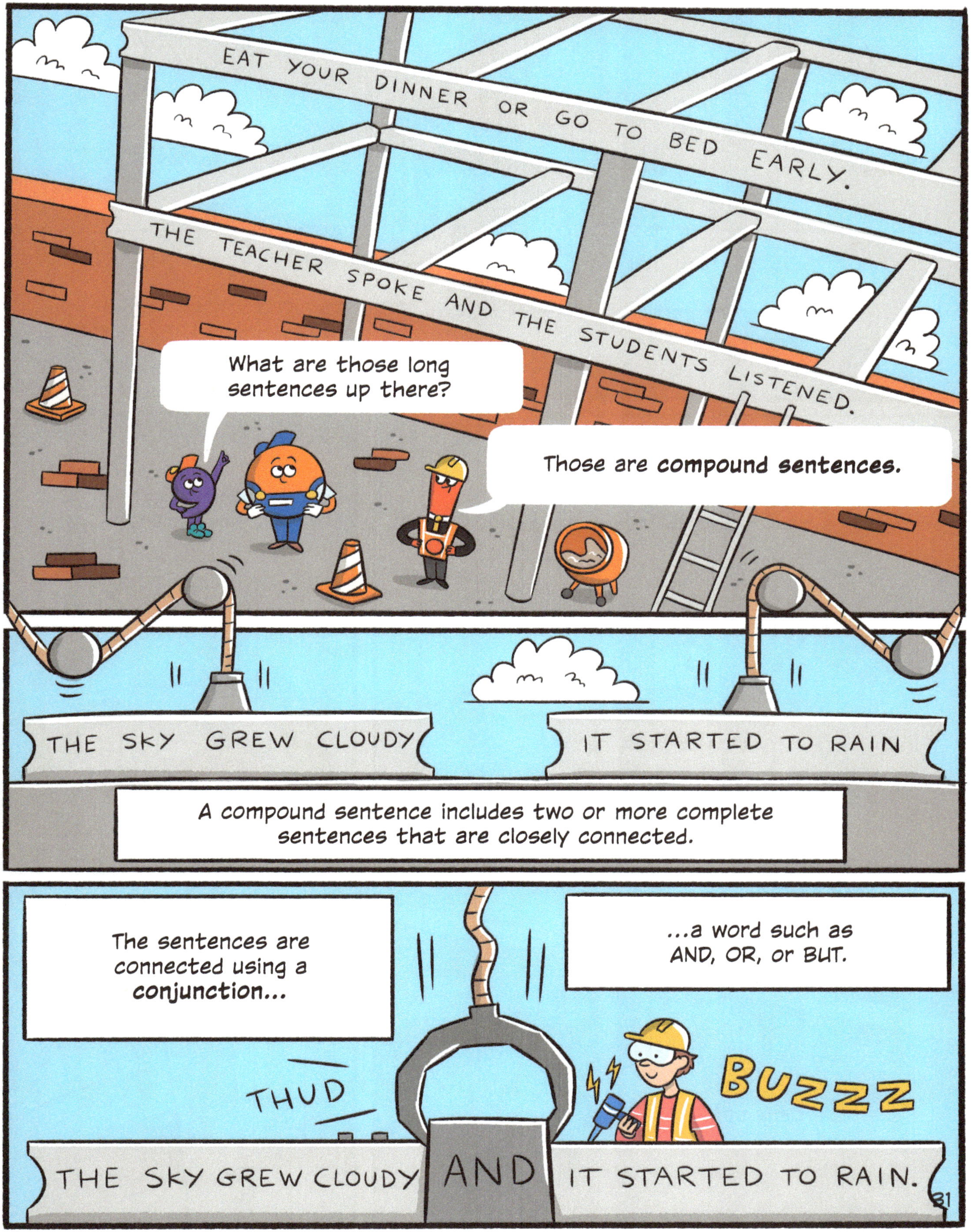

EAT YOUR DINNER OR GO TO BED EARLY.
THE TEACHER SPOKE AND THE STUDENTS LISTENED.
What are those long sentences up there?
Those are **compound sentences.**
THE SKY GREW CLOUDY
IT STARTED TO RAIN
A compound sentence includes two or more complete sentences that are closely connected.
The sentences are connected using a **conjunction...**
...a word such as AND, OR, or BUT.
THUD
BUZZZ
THE SKY GREW CLOUDY AND IT STARTED TO RAIN.

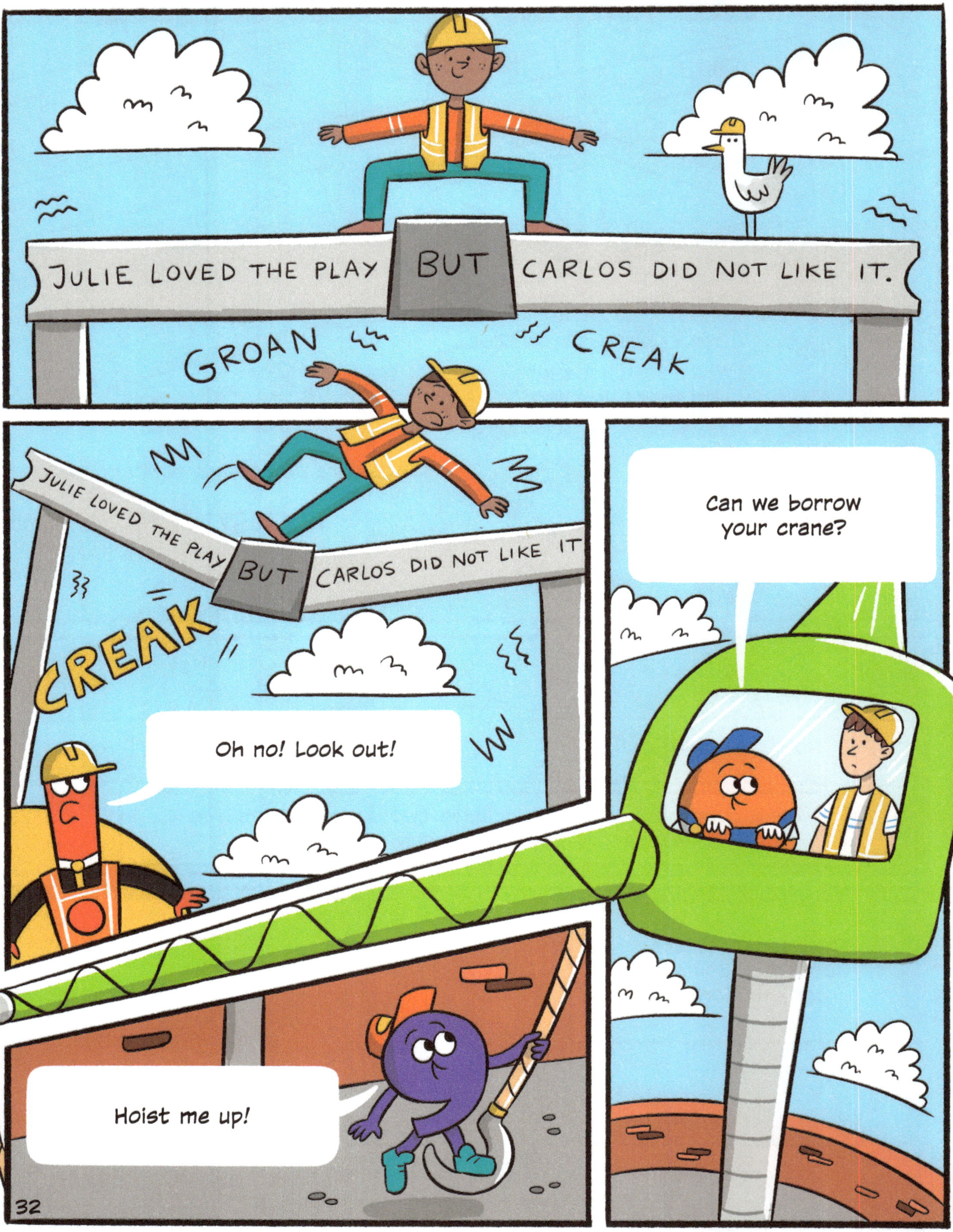

JULIE LOVED THE PLAY
BUT
CARLOS DID NOT LIKE IT.
GROAN
CREAK
JULIE LOVED THE PLAY
BUT
CARLOS DID NOT LIKE IT
CREAK
Oh no! Look out!
Can we borrow your crane?
Hoist me up!

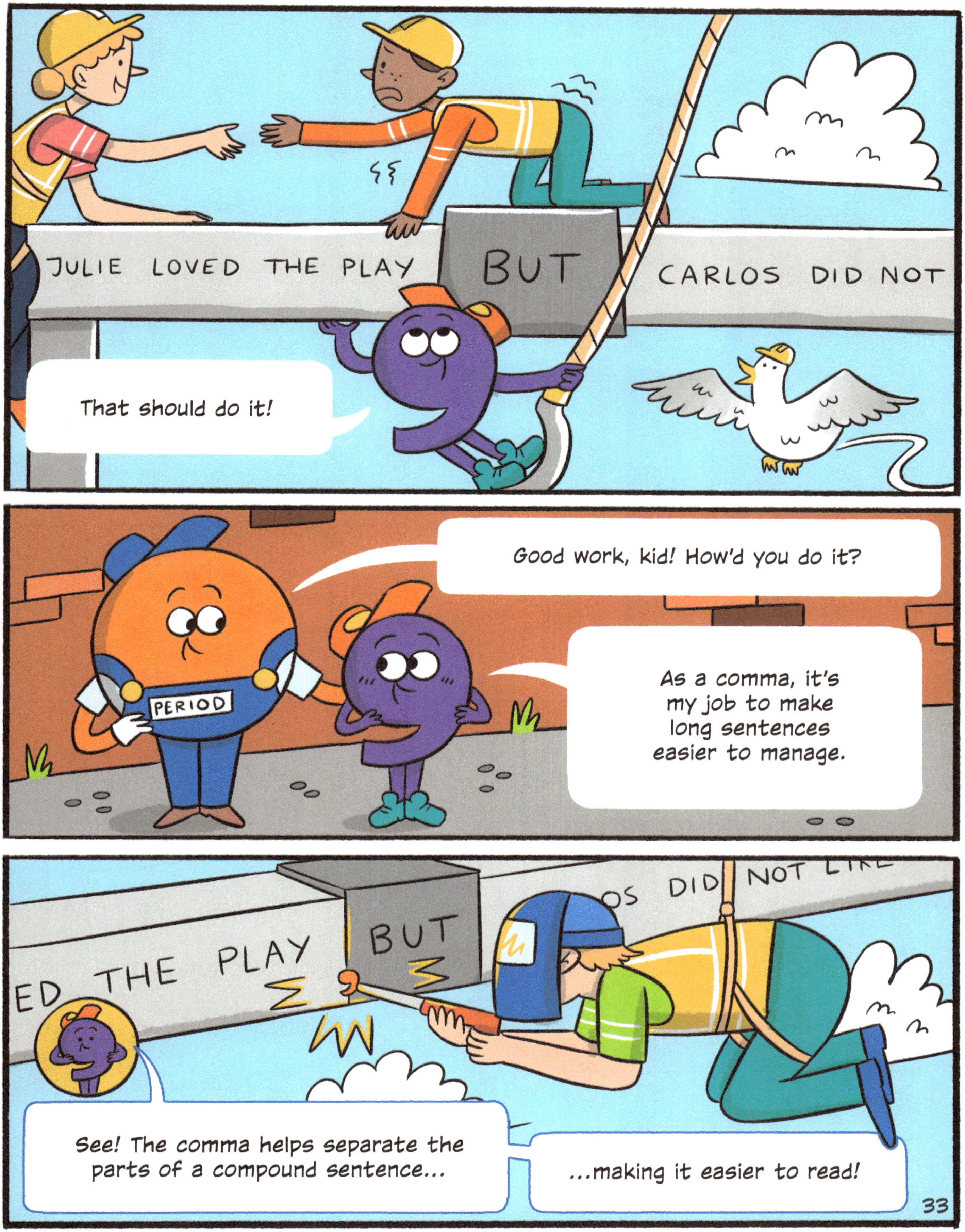
JULIE LOVED THE PLAY
BUT
CARLOS DID NOT
That should do it!
Good work, kid! How'd you do it?
PERIOD
As a comma, it's my job to make long sentences easier to manage.
ED THE PLAY
BUT
OS DID NOT
See! The comma helps separate the parts of a compound sentence...
...making it easier to read!

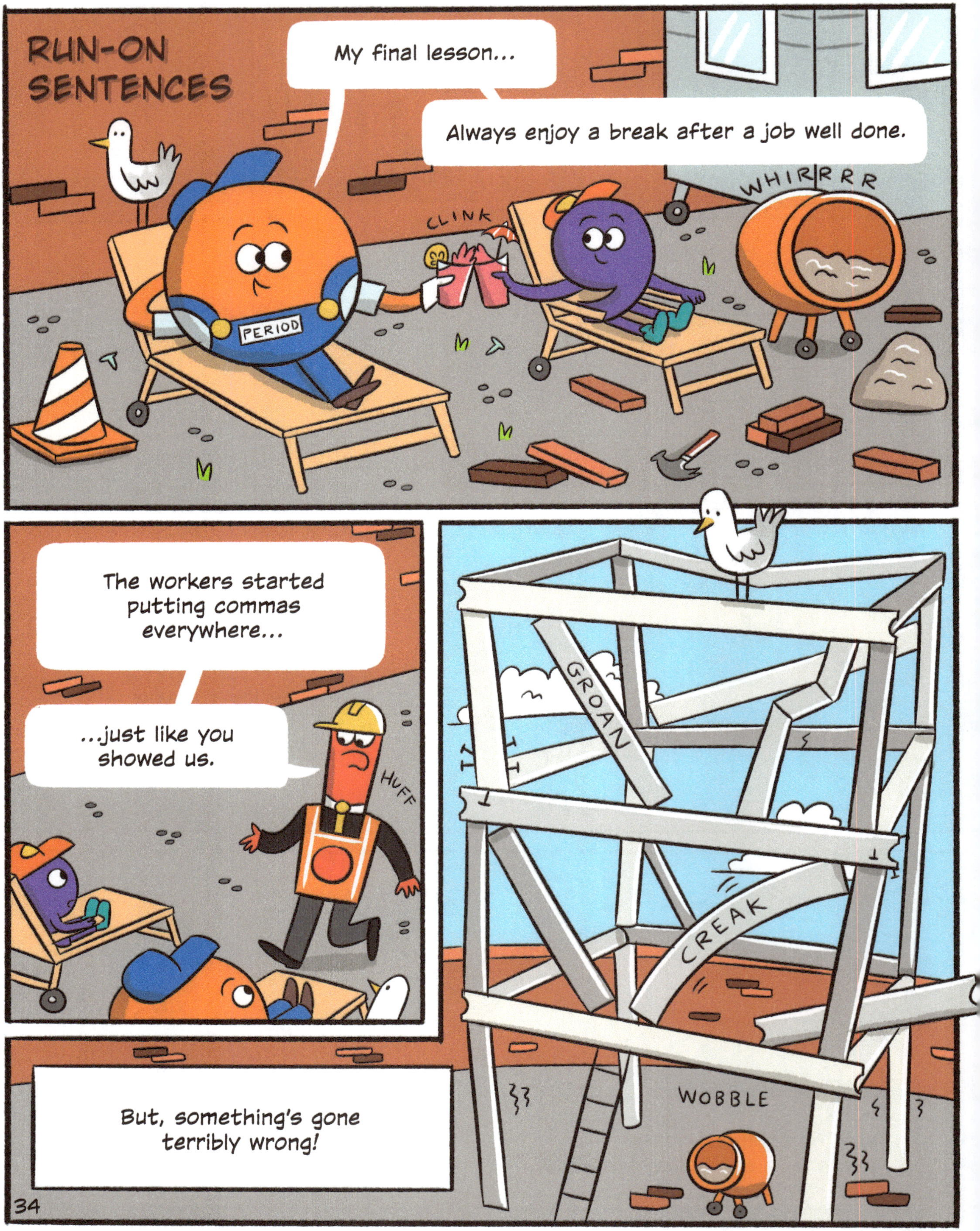
RUN-ON SENTENCES
My final lesson...
Always enjoy a break after a job well done.
CLINK
WHIRRRR
PERIOD
The workers started putting commas everywhere...
...just like you showed us.
HUFF
GROAN
CREAK
WOBBLE
But, something's gone terribly wrong!

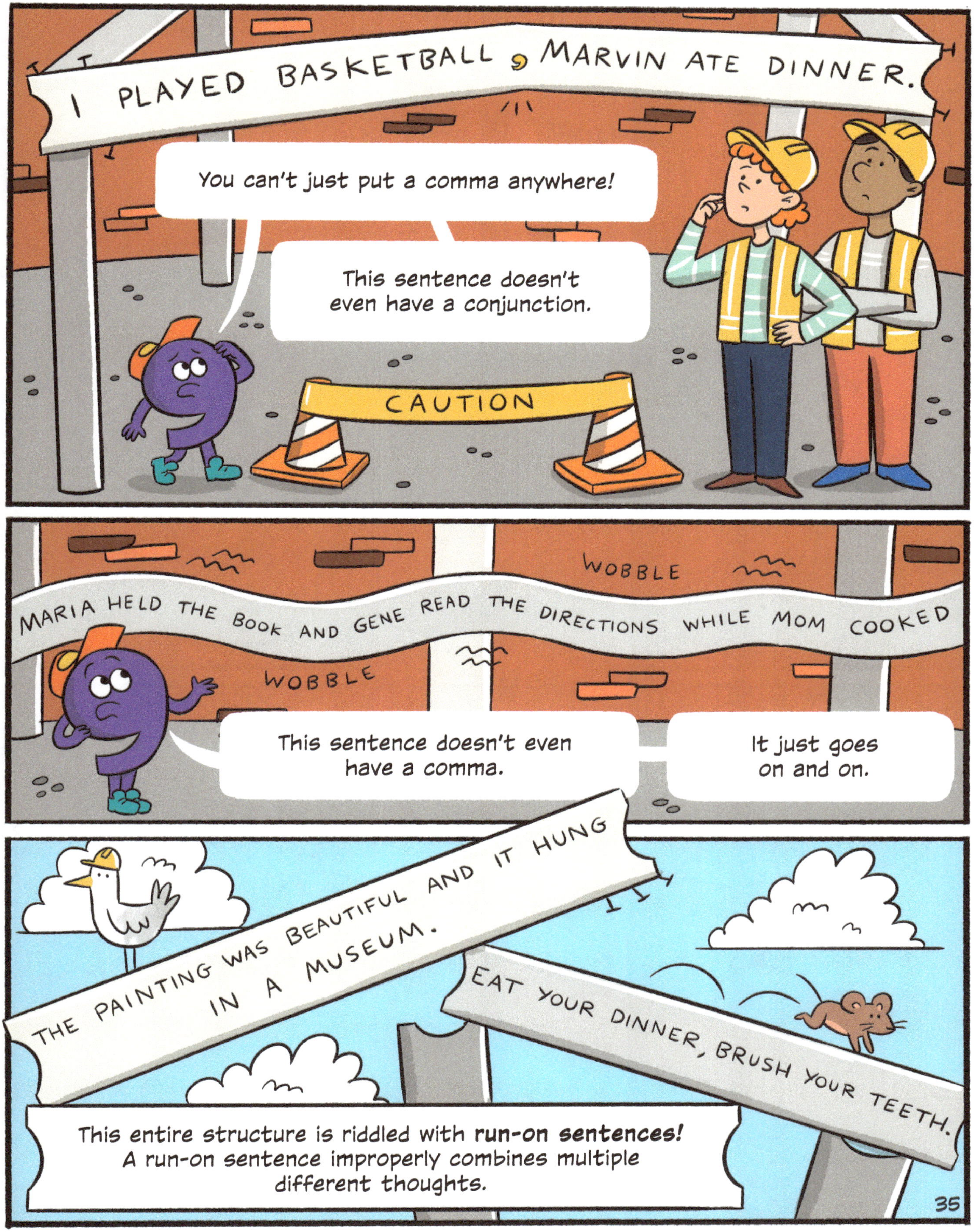
I PLAYED BASKETBALL, MARVIN ATE DINNER.
You can't just put a comma anywhere!
This sentence doesn't even have a conjunction.
CAUTION
WOBBLE
MARIA HELD THE BOOK AND GENE READ THE DIRECTIONS WHILE MOM COOKED
WOBBLE
This sentence doesn't even have a comma.
It just goes on and on.
THE PAINTING WAS BEAUTIFUL AND IT HUNG IN A MUSEUM.
EAT YOUR DINNER, BRUSH YOUR TEETH.
This entire structure is riddled with **run-on sentences!** A run-on sentence improperly combines multiple different thoughts.

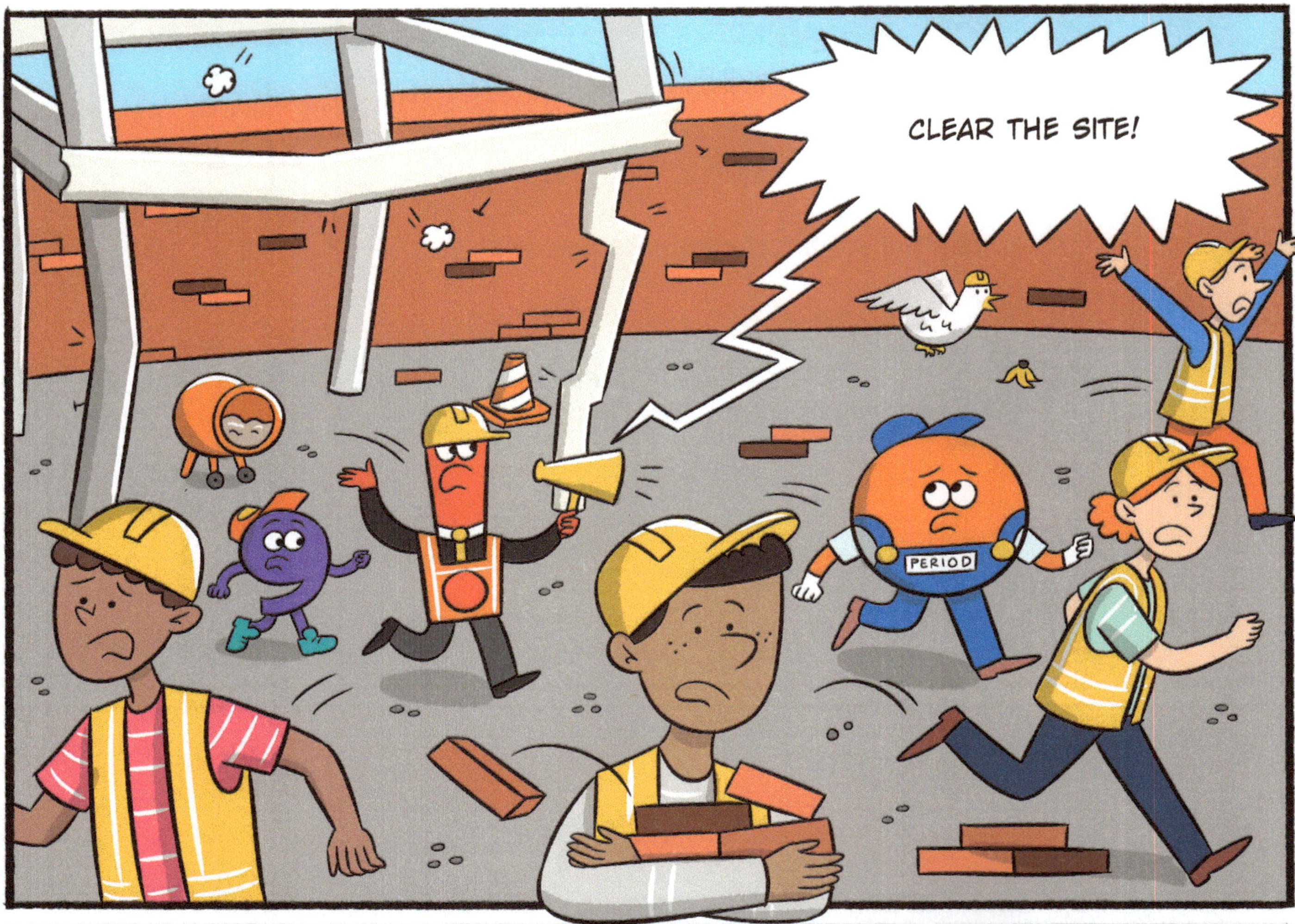
CLEAR THE SITE!
PERIOD

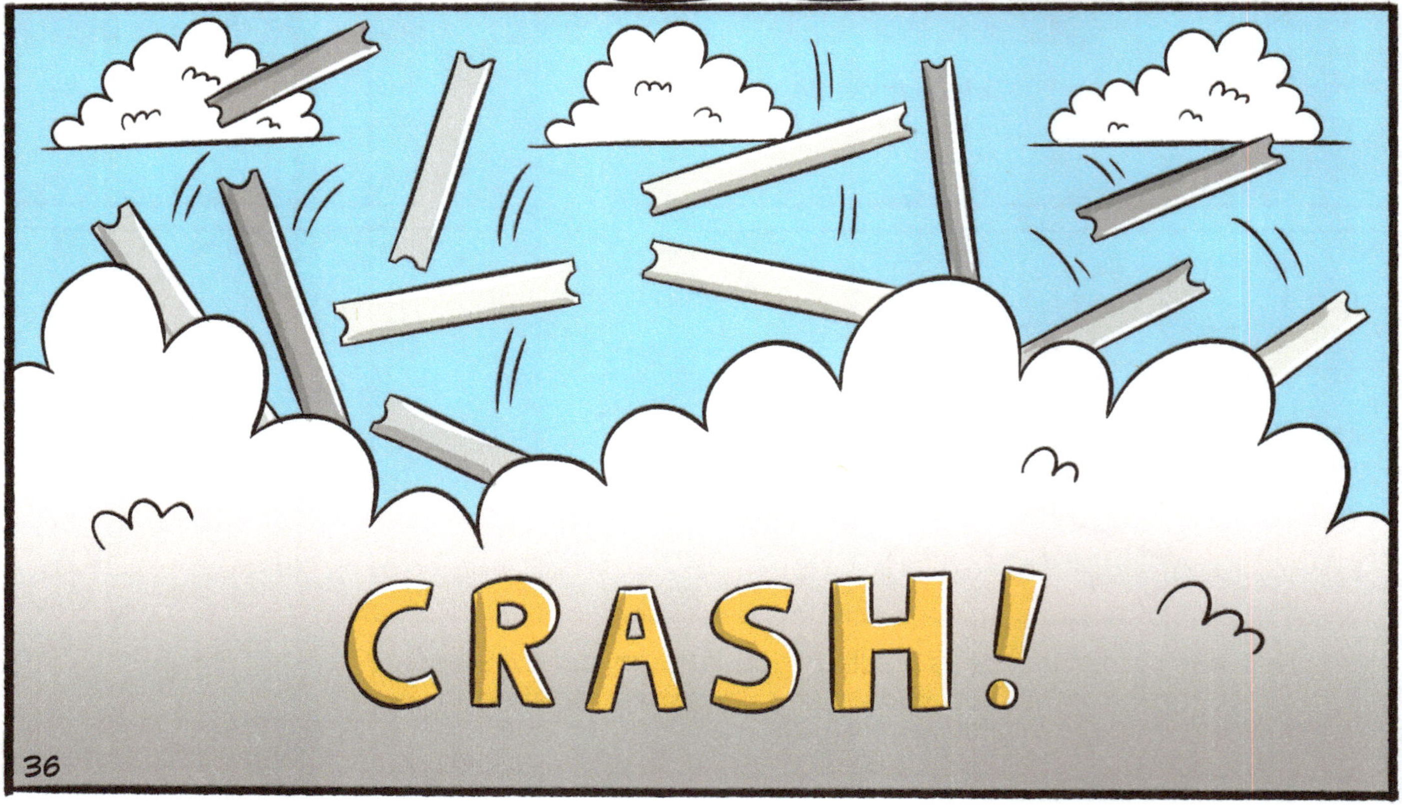
CRASH!

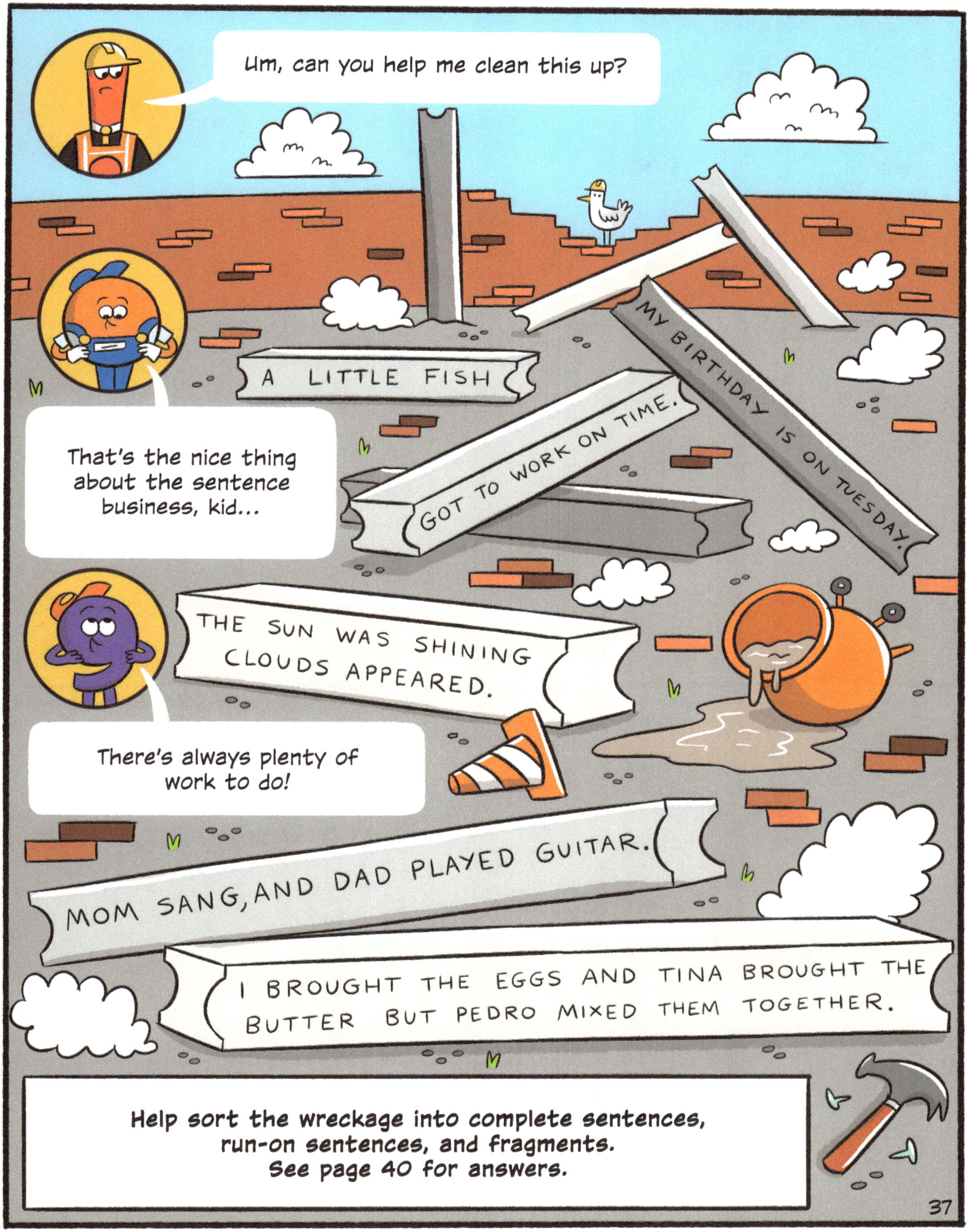
Um, can you help me clean this up?
A LITTLE FISH
MY BIRTHDAY IS ON TUESDAY.
GOT TO WORK ON TIME.
That's the nice thing about the sentence business, kid...
THE SUN WAS SHINING CLOUDS APPEARED.
There's always plenty of work to do!
MOM SANG, AND DAD PLAYED GUITAR.
I BROUGHT THE EGGS AND TINA BROUGHT THE BUTTER BUT PEDRO MIXED THEM TOGETHER.

Help sort the wreckage into complete sentences, run-on sentences, and fragments.
See page 40 for answers.

SHOW WHAT YOU KNOW

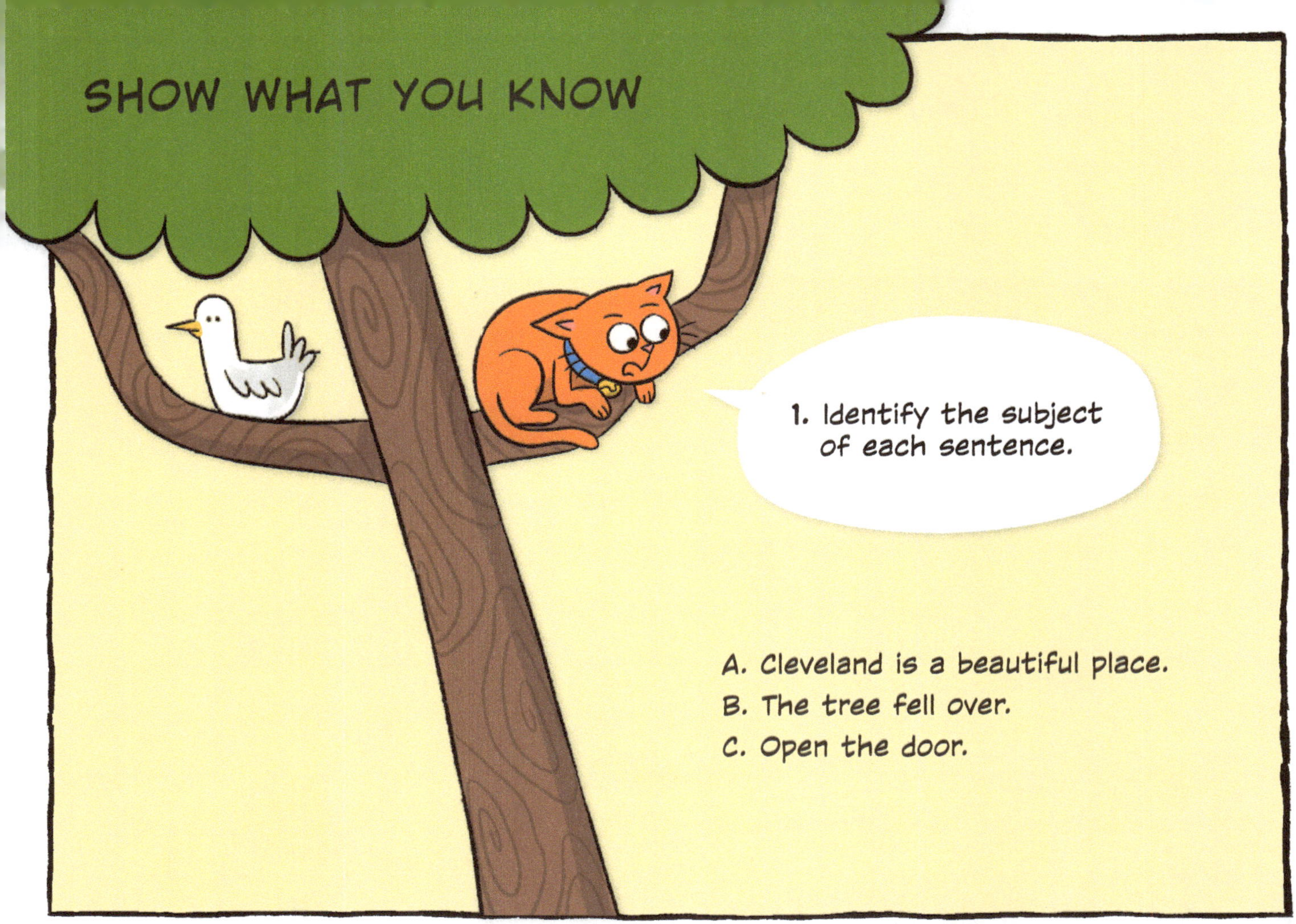
1. Identify the subject of each sentence.
A. Cleveland is a beautiful place.
B. The tree fell over.
C. Open the door.

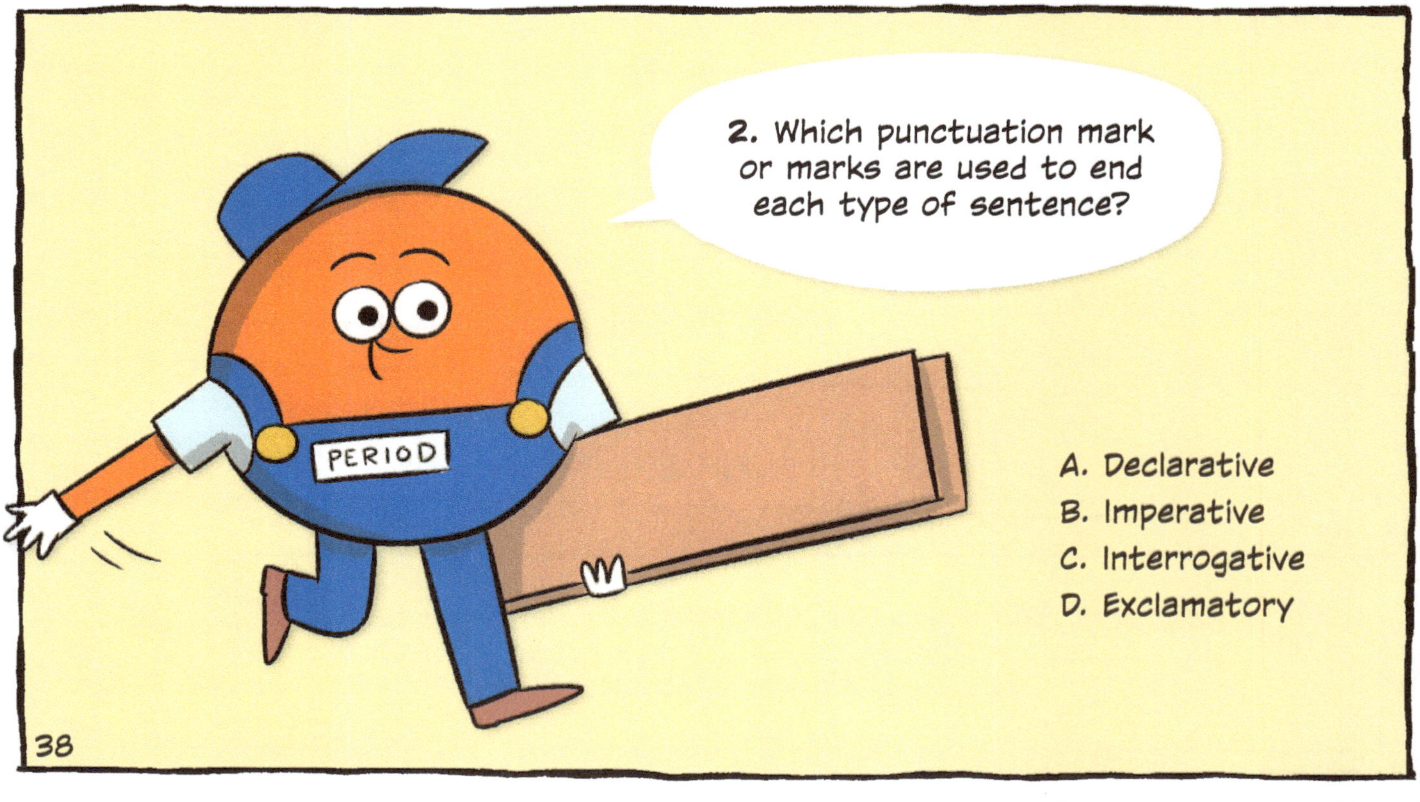
2. Which punctuation mark or marks are used to end each type of sentence?
PERIOD
A. Declarative
B. Imperative
C. Interrogative
D. Exclamatory

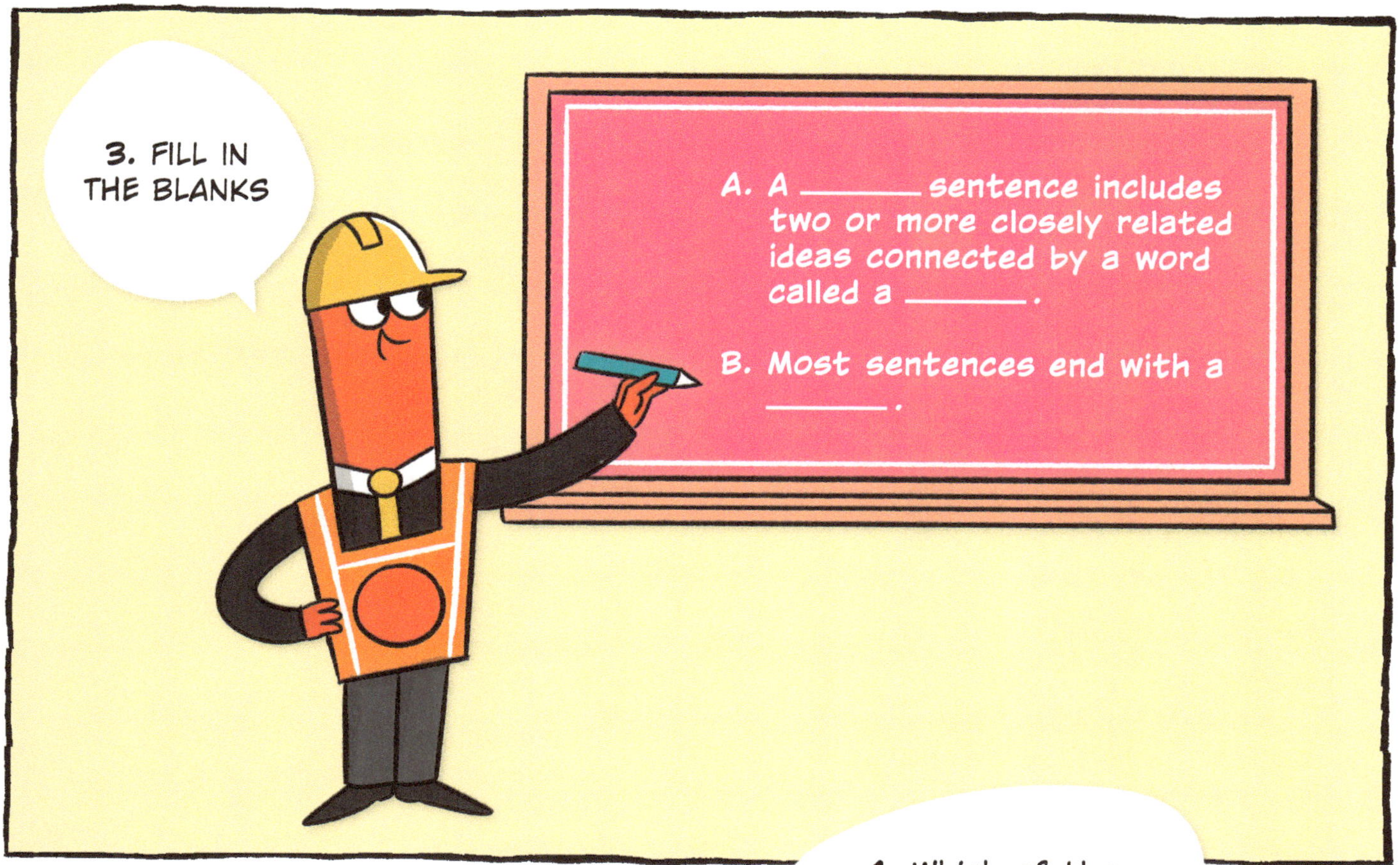
3. FILL IN THE BLANKS
A. A ______ sentence includes two or more closely related ideas connected by a word called a ______.
B. Most sentences end with a ______.

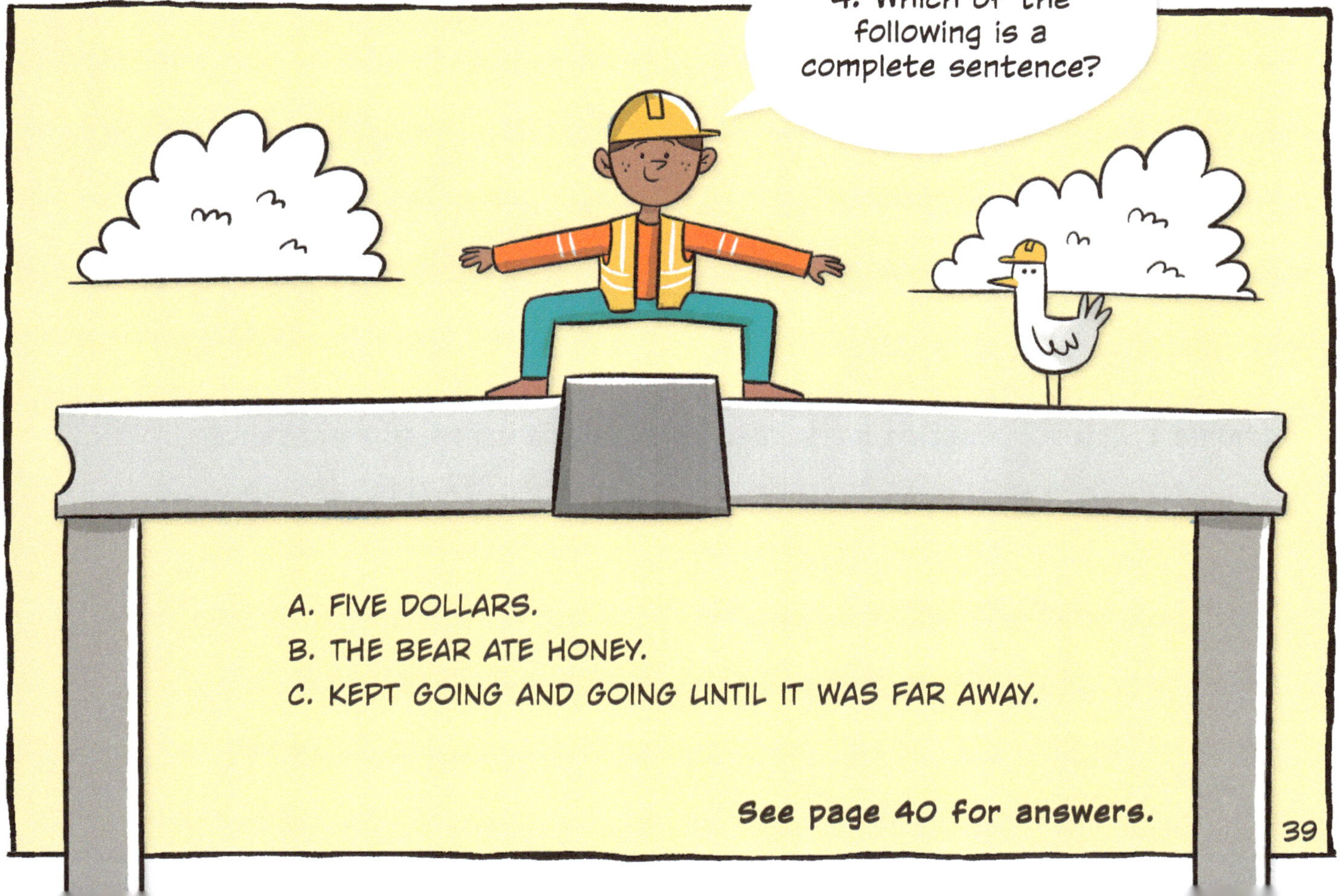
4. Which of the following is a complete sentence?
A. FIVE DOLLARS.
B. THE BEAR ATE HONEY.
C. KEPT GOING AND GOING UNTIL IT WAS FAR AWAY.

See page 40 for answers.

ANSWERS

page 11: THE CAR

page 13: THE TEAM WON THE GAME.

page 19: <u>WHY</u> IS IT SO DARK?

page 27:

MOW THE YARD. -imperative
I AM READY TO GO! -exclamatory
SUMMER IS TOO SHORT. -declarative
WHY DID YOU LEAVE? -interrogative
WHAT TIME IS IT? -interrogative
MY HEAD HURTS. -declarative
QUIT IT! -imperative

page 29: AUNT JENNY

page 30:

THE BIRD I FLEW INTO THE SKY.
THE CAT I SLEPT ON THE COUCH.
THE PIE I WAS DELICIOUS.

page 37:

A LITTLE FISH -sentence fragment
MY BIRTHDAY IS ON TUESDAY. -complete
sentence
GOT TO WORK ON TIME. -sentence
fragment
THE SUN WAS SHINING CLOUDS
APPEARED. -run-on sentence

MOM SANG, AND DAD PLAYED GUITAR.
-complete sentence
I BROUGHT THE EGGS AND TINA BROUGHT
THE BUTTER BUT PEDRO MIXED THEM
TOGETHER. -run-on sentence

SHOW WHAT YOU KNOW ANSWERS
pages 38-39:

1. A. Cleveland
   B. The tree
   C. (You)

2. A. period
   B. period or exclamation point
   C. question mark
   D. exclamation point

3. A. A <u>compound</u> sentence includes
      two or more closely related ideas
      connected by a word called a
      <u>conjunction.</u>

   B. Most sentences end with a
      <u>period.</u>

4. B.

WORDS TO KNOW

comma (,) a punctuation mark used to separate parts of a sentence

compound sentence two or more simple sentences joined by a conjunction

conjunction a word such as and, or, or but that connects the two parts
   of a compound sentence

declarative sentence a sentence that states or declares a fact

exclamation point (!) a punctuation mark that indicates excitement or
   urgency